101 957 951 X

MATHEMATICAL ASSOCIATION

ONE WEEK LOAN

Thr

D1424804

This book was published by The Mathematical Association. Its contents appeared as a supplement to the March 2005 issue of *The Mathematical Gazette.*

Address: The Mathematical Association,
                  259 London Road,
                  Leicester
                  LE2 3BE
                  United Kingdom

Telephone: (+44) 0116 221 0013

Website: www.m-a.org.uk

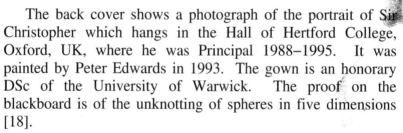

The back cover shows a photograph of the portrait of Sir Christopher which hangs in the Hall of Hertford College, Oxford, UK, where he was Principal 1988–1995. It was painted by Peter Edwards in 1993. The gown is an honorary DSc of the University of Warwick. The proof on the blackboard is of the unknotting of spheres in five dimensions [18].

The photograph on the inside of the front cover shows Sir Christopher in action delivering mathematics at a Royal Institution masterclass.

The Mathematical Association is grateful for being given permission to use these images.

Contents

Foreword

The Mathematical Association began life in 1871 as the *Association for the Improvement of Geometrical Teaching.* It was therefore highly appropriate that Professor Sir Christopher Zeeman, FRS, should choose three-dimensional geometry as the basis of his Presidential Address given in April 2004 at the end of his year as MA President. The text which follows is a greatly expanded version of that Address.

Much could be said about the teaching of geometry in schools nowadays. The amount of geometry currently taught in mainstream curricula is a small fraction of what was done in the past. For many pupils, Euclidean geometry provided a vehicle for developing the principles of proof and logic, as well as containing results of great beauty typified by the geometry of the triangle. The demise of geometry in schools is to be regretted and could arguably be regarded as the main cause of the deterioration in reasoning skills among mathematics undergraduates.

Sir Christopher is without doubt one of the greatest geometers and topologists of his time. The material in his text does not conform to any school curriculum. Rather it is an eclectic mix of topics in three-dimensional geometry which he hopes will prove fascinating and stimulating to abler students in the later stages of secondary education. There is a veritable cornucopia of topics that will provide enrichment either through private study by the reader or by its use in connection with Maths clubs, masterclasses and similar activities. Students and teachers at the tertiary level will also find much to interest them.

Sir Christopher has produced a text which is destined to become a valuable resource. It is to be hoped that it will help to bring about a renaissance in the teaching of geometry in schools in the first half of the 21st century, just as the founders of the *Association for the Improvement of Geometrical Teaching* wished to achieve in 1871.

Adam McBride

MA President 2004-2005

Three-dimensional theorems for schools

Introduction

Geometry is gradually coming back into the school syllabus [17], but so far only 2-dimensional geometry. I would like to make a case for including some 3-dimensional geometry as well, because the latter is vital for describing the world throughout science, engineering and architecture. Higher-dimensional geometry also comprises a major part of modern research within mathematics itself. Also 3-dimensional geometry fosters both our intuitive understanding and our geometric imagination. It teaches us to see things in the round. It also trains us to see all sides of an argument simultaneously, as opposed to algebra and computing which emphasise thinking sequentially.

I give here some examples of 3-dimensional theorems that are suitable for teaching in schools. The statements of all the theorems are geometrical, but the proofs are drawn from a variety of branches of mathematics. In choosing the theorems I have used the following criteria:

- surprising (at first sight)
- intriguing (at second sight)
- essentially 3-dimensional
- noble (capturing the quintessence of some branch of geometry)
- admitting of an elegant short rigorous proof.

The theorems will be grouped under the following topics:

1. Spherical triangles
2. Angles in a tetrahedron
3. Concurrencies in a tetrahedron
4. Perspective
5. Desargues' theorem
6. Regular polyhedra
7. Rotation groups
8. Tessellations and sphere-packings
9. Conics
10. Inversion
11. Cross-ratios
12. Rings of spheres
13. Areas of spheres and volumes of balls
14. Map projections
15. Knotting
16. Linking.

Most of the topics are independent of one another, and can be read separately.

In my Presidential Address I only had time to give theorems from sections 1, 3 and 15, but in this paper I have taken the liberty of including several more topics and theorems in order to illustrate how rich a subject 3-dimensional geometry is, and how accessible it is to young persons at school. To help the reader, and in the spirit of the Association for the Improvement of Geometrical Teaching (the original name of our own

Mathematical Association), I have also included several exercises in Appendix 1, together with their solutions in Appendix 2. At the end of each proof I use the symbol □ to indicate that the proof is complete.

Acknowledgements

I would like to thank all the many mathematicians with whom I have talked about geometry over the years. With regard to this publication, I must thank Gerry Leversha and his team for their editorial role and suggesting several improvements and Bill Richardson for his work in typesetting and drawing all the diagrams.

Notation

Let $\mathbb{R}^2$ and $\mathbb{R}^3$ denote the plane and 3-dimensional space.

Assumptions (stated without proof):

Intersections in $\mathbb{R}^3$

(i)   Two planes meet in a line (unless they are parallel).

(ii) A line meets a plane in a point (unless it is parallel to, or contained in, the plane).

(iii) Three planes meet in a point (unless two are parallel, or the line of intersection of two is parallel to, or contained in, the third).

Two lines in $\mathbb{R}^3$

(i)   Two lines are contained in a plane if and only if they meet or are parallel.

(ii) If two lines are not contained in a plane they are called *skew*, in which case they neither meet nor are parallel.

Definitions of perpendicular (written ⊥) in $\mathbb{R}^3$

(i)   Two lines which intersect are ⊥ if they are at right angles.

(ii) Two skew lines are ⊥ if a line parallel to one and meeting the other is ⊥ to it.

(iii) A line is ⊥ to a plane if it is ⊥ to two non-parallel lines in the plane, and consequently to every line in the plane.

(iv) Two planes are ⊥ if there is a line in one ⊥ to the other.

1. Spherical Triangles

The theorem about the sum of the 3 angles of a triangle being equal to 180° can be generalised to spherical triangles, and then used to give the sum of the 4 solid angles of a tetrahedron.

Definitions: A *great circle* on a sphere is the intersection of the sphere with a plane through its centre.

A *spherical triangle* consists of 3 arcs of 3 great circles.

Let $A°$, $B°$, $C°$ be the angles at the vertices (or more precisely between the tangents to the arcs at each vertex). Let S be the surface area of the sphere and T the area of the triangle.

Theorem 1: (A. Girard, 1629) $A + B + C = 180\left(1 + 4\dfrac{T}{S}\right)$.

Example 1: The triangle shown has 3 right-angles. Meanwhile T occupies a quarter of the northern hemisphere and so $T/S = 1/8$. Therefore

$$180\left(1 + 4\frac{T}{S}\right) = 180 \times \frac{3}{2} = 270 = A + B + C.$$

Example 2: If T gets smaller and smaller compared with S (like a small triangle on the surface of the Earth) then the sum of the angles tends to 180°.

To prove the theorem we need the following lemma.

Definition: Define the *A-lune* to be the region between the 2 great circles through A, and let α denote its area. Similarly let β, γ denote the areas of the *B*-lune, *C*-lune.

Lemma: $\alpha/S = A/180$.

Proof: Looking down on S from above A

$$\frac{\alpha}{S} = \frac{2A}{360} = \frac{A}{180}. \qquad \square$$

Proof of Theorem 1: The 3 lunes cover the whole sphere, but cover the triangle 3 times, which is 2 times too many, and the same with the antipodal triangle. Therefore

$$\alpha + \beta + \gamma = S + 4T.$$

Therefore by the lemma

$$\frac{A + B + C}{180} = \frac{\alpha + \beta + \gamma}{S} = 1 + 4\frac{T}{S}.$$

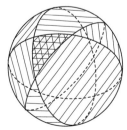

Multiplying by 180 gives the theorem. $\square$

2. Angles of a tetrahedron

Definition: Let $\Delta = ABCD$ be a tetrahedron.

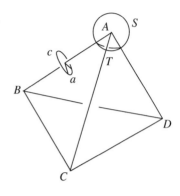

Define the *solid angle* at A to be the ratio T/S, where S is the area of a small sphere, centre A, and T is the area of the spherical triangle cut off by Δ.

Definition: Given an edge AB define the *edge angle* to be the ratio a/c, where c is the circumference of a small circle centred on AB in a plane $\perp AB$, and a is the length of the arc cut off by Δ. The edge angle measures the angle between the faces ABC and ABD in units such that 1 edge angle unit = $360°$.

Theorem 2: In a tetrahedron

       (sum of the 4 solid angles) = (sum of the 6 edge angles) $-$ 1.

Proof: Let S be the area of a small sphere centre A, and let T be the area of the triangle cut off by Δ. Let $k = T/S$. By Theorem 1

       (sum of the 3 edge angles of AB, AC, AD) $= \frac{1}{2}(1 + 4k)$.

Summing over the 4 vertices counts each edge twice and so

     2(sum of the 6 edge angles) $= \frac{1}{2}(4 + 4(\text{sum of the 4 solid angles}))$.

Therefore

       (sum of the 6 edge angles) $= 1 +$ (sum of the 4 solid angles). $\square$

3. Concurrencies in a tetrahedron

We shall generalise to 3 dimensions the following familiar 2-dimensional results about concurrencies in a triangle.

     (i) 3 medians meet at the centroid.

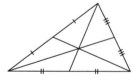

     (ii) 3 side bisectors meet at the circumcentre.

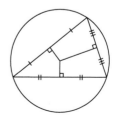

(iii) 3 angle bisectors meet at the incentre.

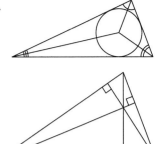

(iv) 3 altitudes meet at the orthocentre.

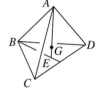

Let Δ = $ABCD$ be a tetrahedron.

Definition: A *median* of Δ is the join of a vertex to the centroid of the opposite face.

Theorem 3.1: The 4 medians meet at the centre of mass G.

Proof: Let $\mathbf{a}, \mathbf{b}, \mathbf{c}, \mathbf{d}$ be coordinate vectors of A, B, C, D. Then $\mathbf{e} = \frac{1}{3}(\mathbf{b} + \mathbf{c} + \mathbf{d})$ is the centroid E of BCD. Let G be the point $\mathbf{g} = \frac{1}{4}(\mathbf{a} + \mathbf{b} + \mathbf{c} + \mathbf{d})$. Then G lies on the median AE because $\mathbf{g} = \frac{1}{4}\mathbf{a} + \frac{3}{4}\mathbf{e}$. Similarly G lies on all 4 medians.

To verify that G is the centre of mass of Δ, note that the line containing BE divides triangle BCD into two subtriangles of equal area. Therefore the plane containing ABE divides Δ into two subtetrahedra of equal volume. Therefore the centre of mass lies in this plane, and similarly in the plane containing ACE, and hence on AE. Similarly the centre of mass lies on all the medians, and hence is G. $\square$

Definition: The *edge bisector* of AB is the plane through the midpoint of, and $\perp$ to, AB. It is the set of points equidistant from A and B.

Theorem 3.2: The 6 edge bisectors all meet at the circumcentre.

Proof: Let S be the intersections of the edge bisectors of AB, BC, CD. Therefore $SA = SB = SC = SD$. Therefore S lies on all 6 edge bisectors, and the sphere, centre S and radius SA, goes through all the vertices. $\square$

Let a, b, c, d denote the 4 faces of $\Delta = ABCD$.

Definition: The edge angle bisector of ab is the plane through CD bisecting the angle between the faces a, b. It is the set of points equidistant from a and b.

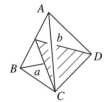

Theorem 3.3: The 6 edge angle bisectors all meet at the incentre.

Proof: Let I be the intersection of the edge angle bisectors ab, bc, cd. Then I is equidistant from all 4 faces, and is the centre of the insphere touching all 4 faces. □

Definition: The *altitude* of Δ through A is the line $\perp BCD$.

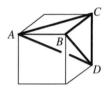

Theorem 3.4: In general the 4 altitudes do not meet.

Proof: It suffices to give a counterexample. Consider Dehn's tetrahedron $ABCD$ inscribed in a cube as shown (Max Dehn, 1900). See Question 2.3. The altitudes through A, D are AB, CD which do not meet.

Theorem 3.5: The altitudes of Δ meet $\Leftrightarrow$ the opposite edges of Δ are $\perp$.

Proof:

$\Rightarrow$ Suppose the 4 altitudes of Δ meet at H.

Then $AH \perp BCD$.

$\therefore$ $AH \perp CD$.

Also $BH \perp ACD$.

$\therefore$ $BH \perp CD$.

$\therefore$ $ABH \perp CD$.

$\therefore$ $AB \perp CD$.

Similarly all pairs of opposite edges of Δ are $\perp$.

$\Leftarrow$ Conversely suppose the opposite edges of Δ are $\perp$.

Let AE be the altitude of Δ through A.

Let BE meet CD in X.

Let BF be the altitude through B of the triangle ABX.

Now $AE \perp BCD$, since it is an altitude of Δ.

$\therefore$ $AE \perp CD$.

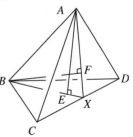

But $AB \perp CD$, given.

∴ $ABE \perp CD$.

∴ $BF \perp CD$.

But $BF \perp AX$, since it is an altitude of ABX.

∴ $BF \perp ACD$.

∴ BF is the altitude of Δ through B.

∴   The 2 altitudes, AE and BF of Δ meet.

∴   All 4 altitudes of Δ meet pairwise. But no 3 are coplanar.

∴   All 4 are concurrent. □

4. Perspective

The rules of perspective show how to paint a 2-dimensional picture of 3-dimensional space. The underlying theorems explain why those rules work. The rules were evidently known in classical times [7], and then forgotten. They were rediscovered in about 1420 during the Renaissance by the architect and artist Filippo Brunelleschi (1377-1446), and were published [1] in 1435 by his friend and fellow architect Leon Battista Alberti (1404-1472). The first rule is that parallel lines in space should be drawn as lines in the picture that converge towards a vanishing point. The rule is illustrated in the following sketch by Jean-Pierre Sharp of the painting of the Annunciation by Domenico Veneziano in 1446, and now in the Fitzwilliam Museum in Cambridge.

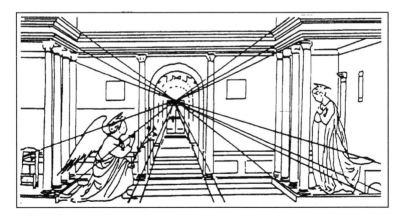

Brunelleschi did not know how to prove this rule mathematically, as in Theorem 4.1 below, because the relevant mathematics was not discovered until some 200 years later, so he proved it scientifically by a cunning experiment, showing that it worked visually. (See [19].)

Definition: Let *P* denote the picture, which it is useful to think of as a pane of glass. Let *E* be the eye, and *A* a point in space. Define the *image A′* of *A* to be the point where the ray *EA* pierces *P*. If *B′* is the image of *B* define *A′B′* to be the *image* of *AB*.

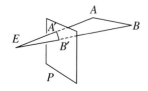

Definition: Given a set *S* of parallel lines in space, define the *vanishing point* of *S* to be the point *V* where the ray through *E* parallel to *S* pierces *P*.

The term 'vanishing point' was introduced by Brook Taylor (1685-1731), whereas Brunelleschi himself merely called it the 'centre point'. Taylor introduced the term because, if the lines of *S* are extended to

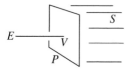

infinity, then *V* is where one would paint the point at infinity. The notion of 'points at infinity' was invented by Johann Kepler (1571-1630) and Girard Desargues (1591-1661). However, I myself prefer the above definition of vanishing point that does not involve infinity.

Theorem 4.1:   All the images of *S*, when extended, go through *V*.

Proof: It suffices to prove that *one* image goes through *V*, for then, by the same proof, they all do.

Let *AB* be one of the lines of *S*. The vanishing point *V* is where the parallel line through *E* pierces *P*.   The two parallel lines *AB*, *EV* determine a sloping plane *Q*. The two planes *P*, *Q* intersect in a line *L*. Now *V* lies in both *P* and *Q* and hence on *L*.

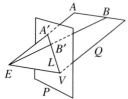

Also *A′* lies in both, and hence on *L*, and the same is true of *B′*. Therefore *A′B′* ⊆ *L* and so, when extended, goes through *V*. □

Drawing a cube: A cube has 3 sets of 4 parallel edges. Therefore the drawing of a cube will have 3 vanishing points *X*, *Y*, *Z*.

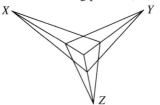

If *E* is the eye then, by the definition of vanishing point, the lines *EX*, *EY*, *EZ* are parallel to the edges of the cube, and hence ⊥ to each other.

Definition: Define a point F to be an *observation point* if FX, FY, FZ are $\perp$ to each other. For instance E is an observation point.

Theorem 4.2: There is exactly one observation point.

Proof: Let E be the eye, and F another observation point. We shall prove that $F = E$. But first we need a lemma.

Lemma: If $FX \perp FY$ then F lies on the circle with diameter XY.

Proof: Complete the rectangle. By symmetry the diagonals bisect each other at O. The circle with centre O and radius OX is the required circle. $\square$

Corollary: F lies on the sphere with diameter XY.

Proof: Spin the circle about the diameter XY. $\square$

Proof of the Theorem: By the Corollary, F lies on the 3 spheres diameters XY, YZ, ZX. Meanwhile E also lies on all the spheres, which guarantees that they meet. The first 2

spheres meet in a circle. This circle meets the third sphere in 2 points. By symmetry (of reflection in the plane of the picture) one of these points lies in front of the picture, and the other is its mirror image behind the picture. But to see the picture one needs to be in front of it. Therefore there is only one observation point and so $F = E$. $\square$

Ambiguous pictures

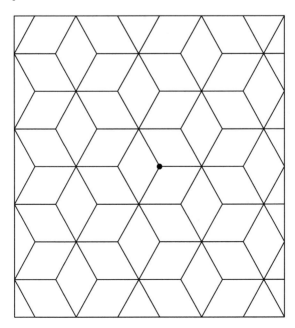

The above diagram has 4 different geometrical meanings.

(i) It is a tessellation of the plane by rhombi. (A *rhombus* is a parallelogram with equal sides.)

(ii) It is the view of the top of a layer of the barrow boy's tessellation of $\mathbb{R}^3$ (see Theorem 8.3 below).

(iii) It is a perspective drawing of a pile of cubes piled up to the right.

(iv) It is a perspective drawing of a pile of cubes piled up to the left.

We draw attention to the last two. The eye tends to get subconsciously locked on one of these two perceptions, which then blocks the other. The question arises how to overcome this block and switch to the other. The solution lies in manipulating the focus of attention, as follows. Focus attention locally on the neighbourhood of the dot in the middle, and blank out everything else to the periphery. For the pile to the left, the dot looks like the corner of a room, whereas for the pile to the right it looks like the corner of a cube. Choose the local interpretation of the dot relevant to the desired perception and then relax. Lo and behold, the chosen global perception will flood into the mind. Focus attention on the other local interpretation and then the other global perception will flood into the mind. The same technique can be used for any ambiguous picture: focus attention upon any detail that is important for the desired interpretation, relax, and the global perception will flood into the mind. (See [20].)

This dialogue between focus of attention and global perception is a visual skill that evolved in animals quite early on, because it gave an evolutionary advantage for the catching of prey and the avoidance of predators. The human species inherited this facility, and we now exploit it for thinking and conversation. If we want to think about some topic we focus attention upon some relevant detail, confident that the whole topic will then flood into the mind. In conversation we draw the listener's attention to some detail with the confident expectation that the whole topic will then flood into his or her mind.

5. Desargues' Theorem

Girard Desargues was one of the founders of projective geometry, which was originally inspired by the perspective of the renaissance painters (see the last section).

Definition: Two triangles are in *point perspective* if the joins of corresponding vertices are concurrent. Two triangles are in *line perspective* if the intersections of corresponding edges are collinear.

Theorem 5: Two triangles are in point perspective if and only if they are in line perspective.

Remark: Surprisingly it is easier to prove this theorem in three dimensions than in two dimensions. Therefore we shall give the 3-dimensional proof here, and assign the 2-dimensional proof as exercises in Questions 5.1 and 5.2.

Proof: Suppose the triangles $T = XYZ$ and $T' = X'Y'Z'$ are in point perspective from V, and do not lie in a plane. Let L be the line of intersection of the planes of T, T'. Let a, b, c denote the planes $VYY'ZZ'$, $VZZ'XX'$, $VXX'YY'$, and let A, B, C denote their intersections with L.

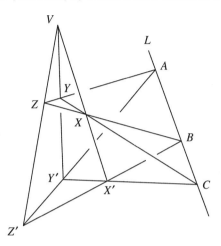

Now YZ, $Y'Z'$ lie in a and so they meet. Also

$$YZ \cap Y'Z' \subset XYZ \cap X'Y'Z' = L.$$

Therefore they meet in $a \cap L = A$. Similarly the other pairs of corresponding sides meet in B, C. Since A, B, C are collinear the triangles T, T' are in line perspective.

Conversely suppose that T, T' are in line perspective. Then YY', ZZ' lie in the plane $AYZY'Z'$, and so they meet. Similarly the 3 lines XX', YY', ZZ' meet pairwise, and are not coplanar, and hence are concurrent. Therefore T, T' are in point perspective. $\square$

6. Regular polyhedra

Plato (427-347 BC) founded his Academy in Athens in about 387 BC, and the platonic solids, or regular polyhedra, were one of the discoveries made at the Academy. The proof that there were only 5 was probably due to Theaetetus (c415-c369 BC). They are described by Euclid [8, Books XI-XIII].

Definition: A *regular* polyhedron is a convex polyhedron that has all its faces congruent to the same regular polygon and has the same number of faces at each vertex.

Theorem 6.1: There are exactly 5 regular polyhedra: the tetrahedron, cube, octahedron, icosahedron and dodecahedron.

Proof: Given a regular polyhedron, the pattern of faces around each vertex contains at least 3 faces; if that pattern is cut open along an edge and flattened out then, by convexity, it will occupy strictly less than 360°. If the faces are equilateral triangles the vertex pattern can contain only 3, 4 or 5 triangles because 6 would occupy the full 360°. Therefore there are 3 cases:

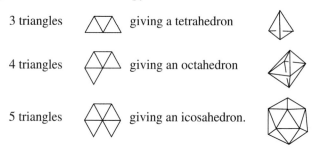

If the faces are squares, there is only one case, namely 3 squares, because 4 squares would occupy 360°:

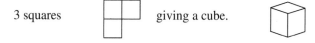

If the faces are pentagons there is similarly only one case:

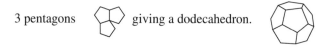

There are no more cases because 3 hexagons (or higher) would occupy 360° (or more). □

Definition: The *dual* of a polyhedron is obtained by joining the midpoints of the faces. Equivalently one can bisect each edge with a dual edge. The advantage of the second definition is that the dual of a dual is the same as you started with.

Examples: (i)   The dual of a tetrahedron is another tetrahedron.
            (ii) The cube and octahedron are duals.
            (iii) The dodecahedron and icosahedron are duals.

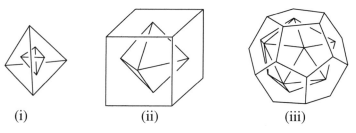

Euler's formula Leonhard Euler (1707-1783) discovered a formula relating the numbers of faces, edges and vertices of a convex polyhedron:

faces − edges + vertices = 2.

See Question 6.1 for a verification that regular polyhedra satisfy this formula.

Associated spheres: Just as a regular polygon in $\mathbb{R}^2$ has 2 concentric circles associated with it, the circumcircle through the vertices, and the incircle touching the edges, so a regular polyhedron in $\mathbb{R}^3$ has 3 concentric spheres associated with it, as follows.

Definitions: Given a regular polyhedron A define the *circumsphere* to be the sphere through the vertices of A, the *midsphere* to be the sphere touching the edges of A, and the *insphere* to be the sphere touching the faces of A.

The corresponding diameters of the spheres are called the *circumdiameter*, *middiameter* and *indiameter*. Notice that the midsphere meets each face in its incircle, and the circumsphere meets the plane of each face in its circumcircle. The diagram shows the 3 spheres associated with a cube.

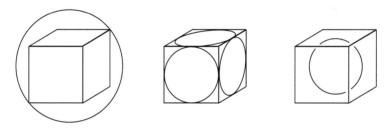

Theorem 6.2: The diameters of the 3 spheres associated with each of the 5 regular polyhedra of edge 1 are as follows:

	circumdiameter, c	middiameter, m	indiameter, i
tetrahedron	$\sqrt{\frac{3}{2}}$	$\frac{1}{\sqrt{2}}$	$\frac{1}{\sqrt{6}}$
cube	$\sqrt{3}$	$\sqrt{2}$	1
octahedron	$\sqrt{2}$	1	$\sqrt{\frac{2}{3}}$
icosahedron	$\sqrt{\frac{5+\sqrt{5}}{2}}$	$\frac{1+\sqrt{5}}{2}$	$\frac{3+\sqrt{5}}{2\sqrt{3}}$
dodecahedron	$\frac{\sqrt{3}(1+\sqrt{5})}{2}$	$\frac{3+\sqrt{5}}{2}$	$\sqrt{\frac{25+11\sqrt{5}}{10}}$

Proof: We give here the proof for the cube, and leave the proofs for the other 4 polyhedra to the reader as Questions 6.3-6.8.

In the cube, the indiameter is the distance between opposite faces, which is the same as the edge of the cube, 1. The middiameter is the distance between opposite edges, which is the same as the diagonal of a face, $\sqrt{2}$. The circumdiameter is the distance between opposite vertices, which is the same as the diagonal of the cube, $\sqrt{3}$. $\square$

Remark about vertex patterns: In the definition of regular polyhedra it is necessary to require that all the vertices have the same vertex pattern otherwise there would be many other examples. For instance the *triangular dipyramid*, which is the union of two tetrahedra glued along a face, is a polyhedron with 6 triangular faces and 5 vertices, but with two different vertex patterns. Each of the top and bottom vertices lies on 3 faces whereas each of the other vertices lies on 4 faces.

Remark about convexity: The condition of convexity is also a necessary condition for the classification. We give an example of a nonconvex polyhedron, beginning with a familiar 2-dimensional example of a nonconvex polygon, the boundary of the Star of David. The latter is the union of dual triangles, T and T', and has 12 edges and 12 vertices, of which there are of two types. The first type are the 6 outer vertices, namely those of T and T'. The second type are the 6 inner vertices, namely the vertices of the hexagon $T \cap T'$. The polygon is not convex because the join of two adjacent outer vertices does not lie inside the polygon.

The analogous 3-dimensional polyhedron is the *stella octangula*, which is the union of dual tetrahedra, T and T'. This has 24 triangular faces and 14 vertices, which are of two different types. The first type are the 8 outer vertices, namely those of T and T', at each of which 3 faces meet. The second type are the 6 inner vertices, namely the vertices of the octahedron $T \cap T'$, at each of which 8 faces meet. The reason why so many faces can meet at a vertex is due to the nonconvexity, because as you go round the vertex pattern, the faces go in and out. The polyhedron is not convex because the join of two adjacent outer vertices does not lie inside the polyhedron.

Going back to convex polyhedra we can extend the classification by allowing the faces to be not all the same.

Definition: A *semi-regular* polyhedron is a convex polyhedron that has faces equal to two regular polygons and all the vertex patterns the same.

Theorem 6.3: There are exactly 15 semi-regular polyhedra having faces with at most 6 edges.

Proof: For the proof see Question 6.10. Meanwhile we list here these 15 semi-regular polyhedra in terms of 6 types. The symbol 3/4 denotes a polyhedron comprised of triangles and squares, etc.

   (i) *Prisms* The *n*-prism consists of two *n*-gons joined by *n* squares. Note that the 4-prism is a cube.

3-prism 4/3   5-prism 4/5 6-prism 4/6

(ii) *Anti-prisms*: The *n*-antiprism consists of two *n*-gons joined by 2*n* triangles. Note that the 3-antiprism is an octahedron.

4-antiprism 3/4   5-antiprism 3/5   6-antiprism 3/6

(iii) *Mitred cube*: To form a *mitred* cube, replace each edge of the cube by a square and each vertex of the cube by a triangle. A *twisted* mitred cube is obtained by rotating the back half through 45°.

mitred cube 3/4   twisted mitred cube 3/4

(iv) *Midedge*: Given a polyhedron *A* define *midedge A* by joining the midpoints of the edges of *A*. Dual polyhedra share the same midedge. Note that the midedge tetrahedron is an octahedron.

midedge cube 3/4   midedge dodecahedron 3/5

(v) *Truncated*: Given *A* define *truncated A* by replacing each vertex of *A* by a face and each face of *A* by another face with twice as many edges.

Note that the truncated cube and dodecahedron are ruled out because they have octagonal and decagonal faces. The truncated icosahedron was named the *buckminsterfullerene* by Sir Harry Kroto in honour of the polygonal roof designs by the architect Buckminster Fuller, and because Sir Harry himself had discovered a new carbon molecule of this shape. It is also the pattern on a football.

truncated
tetrahedron 3/6

truncated
octahedron 4/6

truncated
icosahedron 5/6

(vi) *Snub*: Given *A* define *snub A* by replacing each vertex of *A* by a triangle, each edge by two triangles and each face by a smaller rotated face. Note that these, unlike the rest, are not the same as their mirror images.

snub cube 3/4

snub dodecahedron 3/5

Rhombic dodecahedron: We now introduce an important polyhedron that has all its faces the same, but rhombi rather than regular polygons. Recall that a *rhombus* is a parallelogram with equal sides. The polyhedron will have the same symmetry as a cube and will be useful for tessellations (see Section 8 below).

Definition: A *pyramid* is the join of the centre of a cube to one of its faces.

Definition: A *rhombic dodecahedron R* is a cube with 6 pyramids attached to the outsides of its 6 faces.

Each edge of the cube is the edge of 2 pyramids, and hence of 2 of their triangular faces; these two faces lie in the same plane, since each is at 45° to its base, and so together they form a rhombus, which has that edge as its shorter diagonal. The 12 edges of the cube determine the 12 rhombic faces of *R*. Meanwhile *R* has 14 vertices of two types. The first type are the 8 vertices of the cube, at each of which 3 rhombi meet at their larger angle. The second type are the 6 vertices of the 6 pyramids, at each of which 4 rhombi meet at their smaller angle.

Theorem 6.4: The rhombic faces of R have ratio of diagonals $\sqrt{2}$, and smaller angle $\sec^{-1} 3$ (approximately 70.53°).

Proof: In a cube of side 1 the diagonal has length $\sqrt{3}$, and therefore the sloping edge of a pyramid is $\sqrt{3}/2$. By Pythagoras, the altitude of a sloping triangular face of the pyramid from the centre of the cube has length $1/\sqrt{2}$. Therefore the longer diagonal of the rhombus is $\sqrt{2}$, while the shorter diagonal is 1, and so their ratio is $\sqrt{2}$. Apply the cosine formula to the face of the pyramid:

$$1 = \tfrac{3}{4} + \tfrac{3}{4} - 2.\tfrac{3}{4}\cos\theta.$$

$$\therefore \cos\theta = \tfrac{1}{3}. \qquad \therefore \theta = \sec^{-1} 3. \quad \square$$

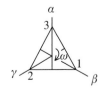

7. Rotation groups

Definitions: A *rotational symmetry* of a polyhedron A is a rotation of A onto itself. The *product* $\alpha\beta$ of two rotations is the composition of α followed by β. The identity map is denoted by 1. The *order* of α is the least positive integer n such that $\alpha^n = 1$. For example a rotation of 180° has order 2, a rotation of 120° has order 3, etc.

Definition: The *rotation group* G of A is the set of rotational symmetries together with multiplication given by composition (one rotation followed by another). Then G is a group because it satisfies the three axioms for a group:

   (i)   associative: $(\alpha\beta)\gamma = \alpha(\beta\gamma)$.

   (ii) unit: $\alpha 1 = 1\alpha = \alpha$.

   (iii) inverse: each α has an inverse α^{-1} such that $\alpha\alpha^{-1} = 1 = \alpha^{-1}\alpha$.

A group is called *abelian* if it is commutative, i.e. for all elements $\alpha, \beta \in G$, $\alpha\beta = \beta\alpha$, but in general rotation groups are not abelian (see Theorem 7.1 below). The *order* of G is the number of elements.

Remark about reflections: Some polyhedra such as the regular polyhedra have reflective symmetries (reflection in a plane) as well as rotational symmetries, and their symmetry group (including both rotations and reflections) is then twice as big as G. However reflections are less intuitive, and so we shall ignore them and confine ourselves to rotations.

Theorem 7.1: The rotation group of an equilateral triangle has order 6 and is called D_3 or S_3. For simplicity, suppose the triangle is horizontal. In the case of D_3, let ω denote a rotation of 120° about the vertical axis through the centroid. Let α, β, γ denote both the altitudes of the triangle, and the 3-dimensional rotations of 180° about these altitudes. In the case of S_3, the rotations are induced by permutations of the vertices 1, 2, 3. The multiplication tables are:

$$
D_3 = \begin{array}{c|cccccc}
 & 1 & \omega & \omega^2 & \alpha & \beta & \gamma \\
\hline
1 & 1 & \omega & \omega^2 & \alpha & \beta & \gamma \\
\omega & \omega & \omega^2 & 1 & \beta & \gamma & \alpha \\
\omega^2 & \omega^2 & 1 & \omega & \gamma & \alpha & \beta \\
\alpha & \alpha & \gamma & \beta & 1 & \omega & \omega^2 \\
\beta & \beta & \alpha & \gamma & \omega^2 & 1 & \omega \\
\gamma & \gamma & \beta & \alpha & \omega & \omega^2 & 1 \\
\end{array}
$$

$$
S_3 = \begin{array}{c|cccccc}
 & 1 & 123 & 132 & 12 & 23 & 31 \\
\hline
1 & 1 & 123 & 132 & 12 & 23 & 31 \\
123 & 123 & 132 & 1 & 23 & 31 & 12 \\
132 & 132 & 1 & 123 & 31 & 12 & 23 \\
12 & 12 & 31 & 23 & 1 & 123 & 132 \\
23 & 23 & 12 & 31 & 132 & 1 & 123 \\
31 & 31 & 23 & 12 & 123 & 132 & 1 \\
\end{array}
$$

Proof: There are two ways of approaching the problem, either in terms of axes of rotation, D_3, or in terms of permutations of the vertices, S_3. We give both approaches because we shall generalise the first to the dihedral groups D_n, and the second to the permutation groups S_n.

D_3 has 6 elements

1 identity: 1

2 rotations of order 3 about the vertical axis: ω, ω^2

3 rotations of order 2 about the altitudes: α, β, γ

To construct the multiplication table it suffices to check experimentally that

$$\omega^3 = \alpha^2 = \beta^2 = \gamma^2 = 1$$

$$\alpha\beta = \omega, \ \beta\alpha = \omega^2, \ \omega\alpha = \beta, \ \alpha\omega = \gamma.$$

The rest of the table can then be completed using the fact that no element appears twice in any row or column.

Meanwhile each rotational symmetry induces a permutation of the vertices, and conversely. Therefore there are 6 permutations:

1 identity: 1

2 3-cycles: 123,132 (where 123 denotes $1 \rightarrow 2 \rightarrow 3 \rightarrow 1$)

3 2-cycles: 12,23,31 (where 12 denotes $1 \leftrightarrow 2$, keeping 3 fixed)

Multiplication is given by the composition of permutations, for example

$$123.12 = 23 \text{ because } 1 \rightarrow 2 \rightarrow 1, \ 2 \rightarrow 3 \rightarrow 3, \ 3 \rightarrow 1 \rightarrow 2.$$

Identify $\omega = 123$, $\alpha = 12$, etc., and it can be seen that the two multiplication tables are the same. Note that this is the smallest non-abelian group. $\square$

Definition of the cyclic groups: Let ω be an element of order n. Define the *cyclic group* C_n to be the abelian group $\{1, \omega, \omega^2, \ldots, \omega^{n-1}\}$. It is the rotation group of a pyramid on a regular n-gon, ω being the rotation through $2\pi/n$ about the vertical axis.

Definition of the dihedral groups: Define the dihedral group D_n to be the rotation group of a regular n-gon. Then D_n has $2n$ elements:

n rotations $1, \omega, \omega^2, \ldots, \omega^{n-1}$ about the vertical axis, and

n rotations $\alpha_1, \alpha_2, \ldots, \alpha_n$ of order 2 about n horizontal axes.

If n is even, half of these axes join opposite vertices, and the other half join the midpoints of opposite edges. If n is odd then each horizontal axis joins a vertex to the midpoint of the opposite edge.

Applications: D_n is the rotation group of the n-prism ($n \neq 4$), and the n-antiprism ($n \neq 3$) (see Question 7.1). D_4 is also the rotation group of the twisted mitred cube (see Question 7.2).

Definition of the permutation groups: The *permutation group* S_n denotes the set of permutations of n objects, which we label with the integers $1, 2, \ldots, n$, together with multiplication given by composition (one permutation followed by another). The *order* of S_n is $n!$, because there are n choices for the image of 1, $n - 1$ for the image of 2, and so on. The identity permutation is denoted by 1. We use the cyclic notation $n_1 n_2 \ldots n_q$ for the q-cycle

$$n_1 \rightarrow n_2 \rightarrow \ldots \rightarrow n_q \rightarrow n_1.$$

Every permutation is the product of 2-cycles, for example $123 = 12.13$ because in the product $1 \rightarrow 2 \rightarrow 2$, $2 \rightarrow 1 \rightarrow 3$, $3 \rightarrow 3 \rightarrow 1$.

Definition: A permutation is called *even* or *odd* according as to whether it is the product of an even or odd number of 2-cycles. The even permutations form a subgroup of order $n!/2$, which is called the *alternating group* A_n.

Technical note: The definition is well-defined, because if $1, 2, \ldots, n$ are the vertices of an $(n-1)$-simplex Δ in n dimensions, then Δ has 2 sides, and a permutation of the vertices induces a map of Δ onto itself that preserves or reverses the sides according as to whether the permutation is even or odd.

Examples

$S_1 = A_1 = A_2$ has 1 element: the identity.

S_2 has 2 elements: the identity, even, and the 2-cycle 12, odd.

S_3 has 6 elements:

    1 identity: even

    3 2-cycles 12, 23, 31: odd

    2 3-cycles 123, 132: even.

∴ A_3 has 3 elements: the identity and the two 3-cycles.

S_4 has 24 elements:

    1 identity: even

    6 2-cycles 12, 13, 14, 23, 24, 34: odd

    8 3-cycles 123, 132, 124, 142, 134, 143, 234, 243: even

    6 4-cycles 1234, 1243, 1324, 1342, 1423, 1432: odd

    3 (2, 2)-cycles 12.34, 13.24, 14.23: even.

∴ A_4 has 12 elements:

    1 identity

    8 3-cycles

    3 (2, 2)-cycles.

S_5 has 120 elements:

    1   identity: even

    10 2-cycles such as 12: odd

    20 3-cycles such as 123: even

    30 4-cycles such as 1234: odd

    24 5-cycles such as 12345: even

    20 (2, 3)-cycles such as 12.345: odd

    15 (2, 2)-cycles such as 12.34: even.

∴ A_5 has 60 elements:

    1   identity

    20 3-cycles

    24 5-cycles

    15 (2, 2)-cycles.

Theorem 7.2: The group A_4 is the rotation group of the regular tetrahedron, and truncated tetrahedron.

Proof: It suffices to prove the theorem for the tetrahedron because the truncated tetrahedron is constructed from it and therefore has the same rotation group.

    Each rotation of the tetrahedron induces an even permutation of the 4 vertices, and conversely. The 8 rotations about the 4 altitudes induce the 8 3-cycles. Call the line joining the midpoints of a pair of opposite edges a *middiameter* of the tetrahedron. (It is in fact a diameter of the *midsphere* touching all the edges.) The 3 rotations of order 2 about the 3 middiameters induce the 3 (2, 2)-cycles. This completes the rotation group, inducing A_4. $\square$

Remark: Note that there is no rotation inducing a 2-cycle.

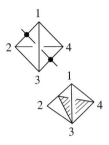

For if there were a rotation inducing the permutation 12, then it would have to be about the middiameter through the midpoint of the edge 12, which also induces the permutation 34, giving the (2, 2)-cycle 12.34. It is true that reflection in the plane ⊥ and bisecting the edge 12 would induce the 2-cycle 12, but we have chosen to ignore reflections.

Theorem 7.3: The group S_4 is the rotation group of the cube, octahedron, mitred cube, midedge cube, snub cube, truncated octahedron, rhombic dodecahedron, and stella octangula.

Proof: It suffices to prove the theorem for the cube, since all the others are generated from it and therefore have the same group.

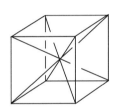
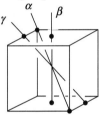

The cube has 4 diagonals joining opposite vertices. Each rotation of the cube induces a permutation of these 4 diagonals, and conversely. The 8 rotations of order 3 about the 4 diagonals, such as α, induce the 8 3-cycles. The 6 rotations, such as β, of order 4 about the 3 indiameters, joining the midpoints of opposite faces, induce the 6 4-cycles, and the 3 rotations of order 2 about the same axes induce the 3 (2,2)-cycles. The 6 rotations, such as γ, of order 2 about the 6 middiameters, joining the midpoints of opposite edges, induce the 6 2-cycles. Hence the 24 rotations of the cube induce the 24 permutations of the 4 diagonals. Therefore the rotation group is S_4. $\square$

Theorem 7.4: The group A_5 is the rotation group of the dodecahedron, icosahedron, midedge dodecahedron, snub dodecahedron, and truncated icosahedron.

Proof: It suffices to prove the theorem for the dodecahedron since all the others are generated from it and therefore have the same group.

The dodecahedron has 12 pentagonal faces, and each face has 5 diagonals. The 60 diagonals form the edges of 5 cubes (see Question 6.8). Each cube has 12 edges, one in each of the faces of the dodecahedron. The diagram shows one of the cubes.

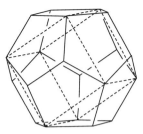

Each rotation of the dodecahedron induces an even permutation of the 5 cubes, and conversely. The diagram below sketches 3 adjacent pentagons, with diagonals labelled by the cubes to which they belong.

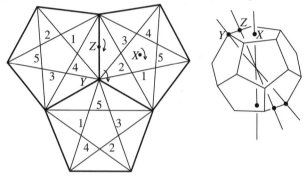

A rotation of order 5 about X induces the 5-cycle 12345. The vertex Y is a vertex of two of the cubes, 1 and 3, and a rotation of order 3 about Y maps each of those two cubes into itself, while inducing the 3-cycle 254 of the other three cubes. A rotation of order 2 about Z induces the (2,2)-cycle 12.34.   Therefore globally the 24 rotations of order 5, 4 about each of the 6 indiameters, the joins of midpoints of opposite faces, induce the 24 5-cycles of A_5. The 20 rotations of order 3, 2 about each of the 10 circumdiameters, the joins of opposite vertices, induce the 20 3-cycles. The 15 rotations of order 2 about the 15 middiameters, the joins of midpoints of opposite edges, induce the 15 (2,2)-cycles. Therefore the 60 rotations of the dodecahedron induce all the 60 even permutations of A_5. Hence the rotation group of the dodecahedron is A_5. $\square$

Remark: We have given examples of the rotation groups C_n, D_n, A_4, S_4, A_5. Felix Klein (1849-1925) [13] showed that these are the only finite groups of rotations in $\mathbb{R}^3$. See Coxeter [6, p. 275] for a proof.

8. Tessellations and sphere packings

Definition: A *tessellation of* $\mathbb{R}^2$ is a covering of $\mathbb{R}^2$ with congruent non-overlapping polygons.

Examples

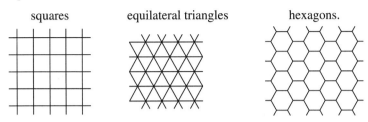

squares   equilateral triangles   hexagons.

There are also tessellations using parallelograms, and indeed using many different shapes including animals; see for instance the well-known work [3] of the artist Maurits Cornelis Escher (1898-1972).

Definition: A *tessellation of* $\mathbb{R}^3$ is a covering of $\mathbb{R}^3$ with congruent non-overlapping polyhedra.

Example: The cubic tessellation has vertices at the integer lattice points (points with integer coordinates).

Theorem 8.1: There is no tessellation using only regular tetrahedra.

Proof: If n regular tetrahedra met at a vertex their solid angles would be $1/n$. But in Question 2.1 we showed that the solid angle of a regular tetrahedron is $\frac{3}{2}\sec^{-1}3 - \frac{1}{4}$, which is irrational. □

Sphere packings: We give 3 examples of packing equal spheres in $\mathbb{R}^3$.

Example 1: *Square packing*: The first layer of spheres is arranged in a horizontal array of rows and columns. The second layer sits in all the hollows of the first layer, and so on.

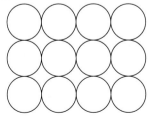

This is also called the *face-centred cubic packing*, because, rotating it through 45°, the centres of the spheres can be located at the vertices of the cubic tessellation together with the centres of all the square faces of all the cubes.

Example 2: *Barrow boy's packing*: The first layer is arranged in a horizontal hexagonal array.

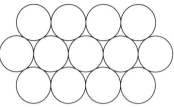

The second layer sits in half the hollows of the first layer. The third layer sits in half of the hollows of the second layer, but not those above the first layer. And so on. The following diagram is looking down from above on a tetrahedron of spheres built according to the barrow boy's packing.

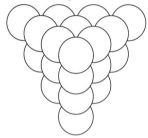

Example 3: *Hexagonal packing*: The first two layers are the same as the barrow boy's packing. The third layer sits in the other half of the hollows of the second layer, exactly above the first layer. And so on. In fact there are an infinite number of different packings by choosing for the different layers either the barrow boy's rule or the hexagonal rule in any order.

Theorem 8.2: The square packing is the same as the barrow boy's packing.

Proof: Consider a barrow boy's tetrahedron of spheres, with 4 spheres along each edge, as shown in the diagram above. The vertical axis is one of the altitudes of the tetrahedron. Now rotate the tetrahedron until one of the middiameters is vertical. The bottom layer is now a row of 4 spheres. The second layer is a 3 × 2 rectangle of spheres. The third layer is a 2 × 3 rectangle, and the fourth layer a row of 4 spheres. In other words we have the square packing. The same argument holds for any size of tetrahedron. Notice that the secret of the proof lies in the fact that the tetrahedron has two types of axes of symmetry, altitudes and middiameters. □

Remark: At first sight it might seem that the barrow boy's packing of spheres is denser than the square packing. In fact each barrow boy's layer is indeed denser than each square layer, but this is compensated for in the square packing by the layers being closer together, because in a regular tetrahedron a middiameter is less than an altitude (the ratio being $\sqrt{3}/2 < 1$). See Question 8.6.

Definition of the tessellation of a packing: A sphere packing induces a tessellation as follows. Each sphere determines a cell of the tessellation by defining the interior of that cell to consist of all points closer to that sphere than to any other sphere.

Theorem 8.3: The cells of the barrow boy's tessellation are rhombic dodecahedra.

Proof: Consider the cubic tessellation of $\mathbb{R}^3$. Imagine the cubes to be coloured alternately black and white like a chessboard. Divide each white cube into 6 pyramids by joining the 6 faces to the centre. Glue onto each black cube the 6 white pyramids on its faces to form a rhombic dodecahedron (see Section 6). This tessellates $\mathbb{R}^3$ with rhombic dodecahedra. For each black cube the midsphere touching its 12 edges at their midpoints also touches the 12 faces of the rhombic dodecahedron at the same points, and furthermore touches the midspheres of the 12 neighbouring black cubes at the same points.

The circumcircles of the black squares on a chessboard in $\mathbb{R}^2$ form a square packing of circles, at 45° to the edge of the chessboard. Similarly the midspheres of the black cubes in $\mathbb{R}^3$ form a square packing of spheres, which is the same as the barrow boy's packing by Theorem 8.2. Let S be one of the spheres, and D the surrounding rhombic dodecahedron. Then S is the insphere of D. Given a neighbouring sphere S' let P be the common tangent plane between S and S', which contains a face of D. Then points closer to S than S' are those on the same side of P as D. Similarly with the other 11 neighbouring spheres, and the other 11 faces of D. Therefore points closer to S than to any other sphere are points interior to D. Therefore D is a cell of the tessellation induced by the barrow boy's sphere packing. Hence the barrow boy's tessellation is the same as the tessellation of rhombic dodecahedra described above. $\square$

Definition: Define the *density* of a sphere packing to be the proportion of the volume occupied by the spheres.

Theorem 8.4: The density of the barrow boy's packing is $\dfrac{\pi}{3\sqrt{2}}$.

Proof: There are two methods. The first is to count the number of spheres inside a large box, which is inaccurate because of the boundary conditions, and then let the size of the box tend to infinity, so that the inaccuracy tends to zero.

The second method is more elegant because it uses the induced tessellation, and compares the volumes of a sphere and its surrounding rhombic dodecahedron, as follows. A black cube has volume 1, while the 6 white pyramids form a white cube of volume 1, and so the rhombic dodecahedron has volume 2. Meanwhile the midsphere of the black cube has diameter $\sqrt{2}$, by Theorem 6.2, hence radius $1/\sqrt{2}$, and hence volume $\frac{4}{3}\pi\left(1/\sqrt{2}\right)^3$.

$$\therefore \text{ density } = \frac{\frac{4}{3}\pi\left(1/\sqrt{2}\right)^3}{2} = \frac{\pi}{3\sqrt{2}}. \quad \square$$

Remark: In 1609 Johann Kepler conjectured that the barrow boy's packing was the densest possible packing of spheres. This conjecture was proved in 1998 by Thomas Hales [10].

9. Conics

Definition: A *circular cone* is the surface obtained by joining a horizontal circle to a vertex vertically above the centre of the circle. The vertex is called the *centre* of the cone. A *conic* is the intersection of a circular cone with a plane not through its centre.

Conics were discovered by Menaechmus at Plato's Academy in about 340 BC. Then Euclid (c330-c275 BC) wrote four books on conics, now lost, and the great geometer Apollonius (c260-190 BC) absorbed these and developed the whole theory in eight more books. The proof we give in Theorem 9.1 below is due to G. P. Dandelin in 1822.

Let α be the semi-angle of the cone, and β the angle between the axis of the cone and the plane. There are 3 cases according as to whether α is less than, equal to, or greater than β.

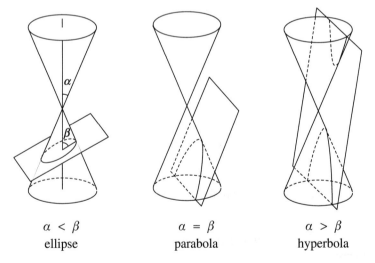

$\alpha < \beta$	$\alpha = \beta$	$\alpha > \beta$
ellipse	parabola	hyperbola

Definitions: An *ellipse* is the locus of a point in the plane the sum of whose distances from 2 points (called *foci*) is constant. A *hyperbola* is the locus of a point in the plane the difference of whose distances from 2 foci is constant. A *parabola* is the locus of a point in the plane equidistant from a point (the *focus*) and a line (the *directrix*).

We shall prove the elliptic case, and set the other two as Questions 9.2 - 9.5.

Theorem 9.1: If $\alpha < \beta$ the conic is an ellipse.

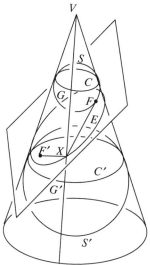

Proof: Let E be the intersection between the cone and plane. Let S, S' be the spheres above and below the plane touching both cone and plane. Let C, C' be the horizontal circles where the spheres touch the cone, and let F, F' be the points where they touch the plane. Let V be the vertex of the cone. Given $X \in E$, let G, G' be the points where VX meets C, C'. Then

$$XF = XG, \text{ being tangents from } X \text{ to } S.$$

$$XF' = XG', \text{ being tangents from } X \text{ to } S'.$$

$$\therefore XF + XF' = XG + XG'$$

$$= GG'$$

$$= \text{constant, independent of } X.$$

Therefore E, the locus of X, is an ellipse, with foci F, F'. $\square$

Some readers may be more familiar with the description of an ellipse by an equation, and so in the next theorem we deduce that equation from the definition above.

Theorem 9.2: If the ellipse has major, minor semi-axes a, b then, with appropriate choice of axes, it has the equation

$$\left(\frac{x}{a}\right)^2 + \left(\frac{y}{b}\right)^2 = 1.$$

Proof:

With origin O, take x and y-axes along the major and minor semi-axes of the ellipse. Let F, F' be the foci at $(\pm c, 0)$. Let $A = (a, 0)$ and $B = (0, b)$ be the ends of the major and minor axes. Let X be a point on the ellipse.

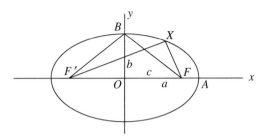

When $X = A$ then $AF + AF' = (a - c) + (a + c) = 2a$.
When $X = B$ then $BF + BF' = 2BF = 2a$, by constancy.

$$\therefore BF = a. \qquad \therefore a^2 - c^2 = b^2.$$

If $X = (x, y)$ then by constancy

$$\sqrt{(x - c)^2 + y^2} + \sqrt{(x + c)^2 + y^2} = 2a.$$

Squaring:

$$\left(x^2 + y^2 + c^2 - 2cx\right) + \left(x^2 + y^2 + c^2 + 2cx\right) +$$
$$2\sqrt{(x^2 + y^2 + c^2 - 2cx)(x^2 + y^2 + c^2 + 2cx)} = 4a^2$$

$$\therefore \sqrt{(x^2 + y^2 + c^2)^2 - 4c^2x^2} = 2a^2 - \left(x^2 + y^2 + c^2\right).$$

Squaring:

$$\left(x^2 + y^2 + c^2\right)^2 - 4c^2x^2 = 4a^4 - 4a^2\left(x^2 + y^2 + c^2\right) + \left(x^2 + y^2 + c^2\right)^2$$

$$\therefore a^2\left(x^2 + y^2 + c^2\right) - c^2x^2 = a^4$$

$$\therefore \left(a^2 - c^2\right)x^2 + a^2y^2 = a^2\left(a^2 - c^2\right)$$

$$\therefore b^2x^2 + a^2y^2 = a^2b^2$$

$$\therefore \left(\frac{x}{a}\right)^2 + \left(\frac{y}{b}\right)^2 = 1. \ \square$$

10. Inversion in a sphere

Inversion in a sphere is a generalisation to $\mathbb{R}^3$ of the more familiar inversion in a circle in $\mathbb{R}^2$. It is basically a tool, useful for proving other theorems, such as those in Sections 12 and 14.

Definition: Define *inversion in a sphere S*, with centre O and radius k, (or, more briefly, *inversion in the point O*) to be the map $f : \{\mathbb{R}^3 - O\} \to \{\mathbb{R}^3 - O\}$ given by $X \to X'$, where X' is the point on the ray OX such that $OX.OX' = k^2$. (A *ray* is a halfline beginning at O.)

Note that f leaves points of S fixed, and interchanges the inside and outside of S. Note also that f is an *involution* because $f^2 = 1$, and so $f^{-1} = f$. In terms of topology, f is a *homeomorphism*, in other words a continuous one-to-one map with continuous inverse.

Theorem 10.1: The inversion f maps:
  (i) planes through O to themselves;
  (ii) planes not through O to spheres through O, and vice versa;
  (iii) the tangent plane at N to the sphere diameter ON, and vice versa;
  (iv) spheres not through O to spheres not through O.

Proof: (i) f maps a ray through O to itself, and hence planes through O to themselves.
(ii) Given a plane Π not through O, let ON be the $\perp$ from O onto Π. Given $X \in \Pi$, let f map $X \to X', N \to N'$. Then

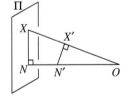

$$OX.OX' = k^2 = ON.ON'$$

$$\therefore \frac{OX'}{ON'} = \frac{ON}{OX}.$$

Therefore triangles $OX'N'$, ONX are similar, having the angle at O in common.

$$\therefore \angle OX'N' = \angle ONX = 90°.$$

Therefore X' lies on the sphere diameter ON'.
Therefore f maps Π to this sphere. And vice versa since $f^{-1} = f$.
(iii) If Π is the tangent plane to S at N then $N' = N$. Therefore f maps Π to the sphere diameter ON.

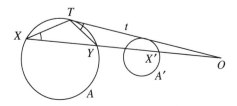

(iv) Given a sphere A let OT be a tangent to A, of length t say. Let A' be the sphere A shrunk towards (or expanded away from) O by a factor k^2/t^2. We shall prove $f(A) = A'$. Given $X \in A$, let Y be the other intersection of OX with A, and let X' be the image of Y under the shrinkage. Then $\angle OXT = \angle OTY$ because the angle between chord and tangent of a circle equals the angle subtended by the chord in the opposite segment (see Question 10.1). Therefore the triangles OXT, OTY are similar, having the angle at O in common.

$$\therefore \frac{OX}{OT} = \frac{OT}{OY}$$

$$\therefore OX.OY = OT^2 = t^2$$

But $\dfrac{OX'}{OY} = \dfrac{k^2}{t^2}$, by the shrinkage.

Multiply the last two lines together: $OX.OX' = k^2$.

$$\therefore f(X) = X' \text{ and so } f(A) = A'. \ \square$$

Corollary 10.2: The inversion f maps:
   (i)   lines through O to themselves,
  (ii)   lines not through O to circles through O, and vice versa,
 (iii)   circles not through O to circles not through O.

Proof: (i) f maps rays through O to themselves, and hence lines also.

(ii) A line not through O is the intersection of 2 planes not through O. Their images are 2 spheres through O, which intersect in a circle through O.

(iii) A circle not through O is the intersection of 2 spheres not through O. Their images are two spheres not through O, which intersect in a circle not through O. $\square$

Corollary 10.3: If the inversion maps a plane (or line) at distance d from O to the sphere (or circle) of radius r then $2rd = k^2$.

Proof: If OX is the $\perp$ from O to the plane (or line) and OX' the diameter of the sphere (or circle) then X' is the image of X, and so

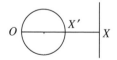

$$2rd = d.2r = OX.OX' = k^2. \ \square$$

Definition: We say a map is *conformal* if it preserves angles. Recall that the *angle* between two curves meeting at P is defined to be the angle between their tangents at P.

Theorem 10.4: Inversion is conformal.

Proof: Suppose A, B are 2 lines not through O, meeting at P. Under inversion in O let A', B' be their image circles through O and through P', the image of P.

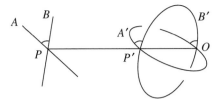

The tangents at O to A', B' are parallel to A, B. Therefore

angle between A, B at P = angle between tangents to A', B' at O

= angle between A', B' at O, by definition

= angle between A', B' at P', by symmetry

(the symmetry of reflection in the plane $\perp$ and bisecting OP'). Hence angles are preserved. $\square$

Corollary 10.5: Inversion preserves tangency.

Proof: Touching is equivalent to the following condition: surfaces A, B touch at P if, given any curve α in A through P, there exists a curve β in B through P at zero angle to α. By Theorem 10.4 inversion preserves angles, and hence the condition, and hence touching. $\square$

11. Cross-ratio

Just as distance is the main invariant of euclidean geometry so cross-ratio is the main invariant of projective geometry. Like inversion in the last section, we regard this primarily as a tool for proving other theorems, such as Theorem 12.6. For a fuller treatment see Coxeter [6].

Definitions: Given 4 points A, B, C, D on a line define the *cross-ratio*

$$(ABCD) = \frac{AB.CD}{AD.CB}.$$

Given 4 lines through a point O define the *cross-ratio*

$$O(ABCD) = \frac{\sin \angle AOB. \sin \angle COD}{\sin \angle AOD. \sin \angle COB}.$$

Theorem 11.1: $(ABCD) = O(ABCD)$.

Proof: Let h be the distance from O to the line $ABCD$.

$$\tfrac{1}{2}h.AB = \text{area of triangle } AOB = \tfrac{1}{2}OA.OB \sin \angle AOB.$$

$$\therefore AB = \frac{OA.OB}{h} \sin \angle AOB.$$

$$\therefore (ABCD) = \frac{(OA.OB \sin \angle AOB)(OC.OD \sin \angle COD)}{(OA.OD \sin \angle AOD)(OC.OB \sin \angle COB)} = O(ABCD). \ \square$$

Definition: Given two lines L, L' and a point O, the *projection* $L \to L'$ from O is defined by the rays from O.

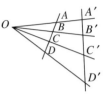

Corollary 11.2: Projection preserves cross-ratio.

Proof: From O project 4 points A, B, C, D on a line to 4 points A', B', C', D' on another line. Then

$$(ABCD) = O(ABCD) = O(A'B'C'D') = (A'B'C'D'). \quad \square$$

Definition: Given 4 points A, B, C, D on a circle define the *cross-ratio* $(ABCD)$ to be $O(ABCD)$ for any other point O on the circle.

Note that the cross-ratio is independent of the choice of O because if O' is another point on the circle then either $\angle AO'B = \angle AOB$, or $\angle AO'B = 180° - \angle AOB$, and so $\sin \angle AO'B = \sin \angle AOB$. Hence the cross-ratio is the same.

Theorem 11.3: Inversion preserves cross-ratio.

Proof: Given points A, B, C, D on a line L, suppose they are inverted in O to points A', B', C', D' on the circle L'. Then by Theorem 11.1 and by definition

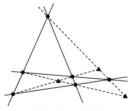

$$(ABCD) = O(ABCD)$$

$$= O(A'B'C'D')$$

$$= (A'B'C'D') \text{ on } L'. \quad \square$$

Definition: A set of points A, B, C, D on a line or circle is called *harmonic* if $(ABCD) = -1$. We sometimes say that A, C separate harmonically B, D.

Example: Define a *complete quadrilateral* to consist of 4 lines meeting in 6 vertices (shown as dots).

The 3 diagonals (shown dashed) are the joins of those quadrilateral vertices not already joined, and they meet in 3 diagonal vertices (shown as little triangles). Then on any diagonal the 2 diagonal vertices separate harmonically the 2 quadrilateral vertices (see Question 11.1).

Lemma: A, B, C, ∞ is harmonic if and only if B is the midpoint of AC.

Proof: As $D \to \infty$, $CD/AD \to 1$, and so

$$(ABCD) \to \frac{AB}{CB}.$$

If $AB/CB = -1$ then $AB = -CB = BC$, and conversely. $\quad \square$

Theorem 11.4: If B is the midpoint of AC on a line L, and inversion in O maps A, B, C to A', B', C' on the circle L' through O then A', B', C', O are harmonic on L'.

Proof: The tangent to L' at O meets L at ∞.

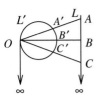

$$(A'B'C'O) = O(A'B'C'O), \text{ by definition}$$
$$= (ABC\infty), \text{ by projection on } L,$$
$$= -1, \text{ by the Lemma.}$$

(Here $O(O)$ denotes the tangent at O.) $\square$

12. Rings of spheres

Definition: A *ring* of spheres is an ordered set of spheres such that each touches the next, and the last touches the first. If there are q spheres, where q is a positive integer, then it is called a *q-ring*.

Note that the spheres may not be the same size, and their centres may not be in the same plane.

Definition: Two rings α, β *interlock* if each sphere of α touches each sphere of β.

Interlocking rings have been studied by Frederick Soddy [16], H S M Coxeter [5] and Michael Fox [9]. I would like to thank the latter for introducing me to the subject.

Theorem 12.1: If a p-ring interlocks a q-ring then $1/p + 1/q = 1/2$.

Proof: Invert in the point of contact between the first two spheres of the p-ring. Let $\alpha = (A_1, \dots, A_p)$, $\beta = (B_1, \dots, B_q)$ denote the images of the p-ring, q-ring. By Theorem 10.1(ii) A_1, A_2 are parallel planes, which it is convenient to think of as horizontal. Meanwhile by Theorem 10.1(iv) and Corollary 10.5 the rest $A_3, \dots, A_p$ are a chain of spheres, each touching the next, with A_3 touching the plane A_2, and A_p touching the plane A_1.

All the spheres $B_1, \dots, B_q$ touch the planes A_1, A_2 and are therefore all the same size, of radius r say. Also they all touch A_3, and therefore form a circle of spheres around A_3. Let b denote the circle containing their points of contact, of centre P and radius R say. If $\phi = 360/2q = 180/q$ then $\tan\phi° = r/R$.

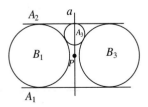

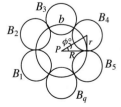

Let a be the vertical line through P, which goes through the centres of $A_3, \dots A_p$ and all their points of contact.

Now invert in the sphere with centre O, the point of contact of B_1 and B_2, and radius k say. Let $\alpha' = (A_1', \dots, A_p')$, $\beta' = (B_1', \dots, B_q')$ be the images of α, β. Then B_1', B_2' are parallel planes each at a distance r' from O, where $2rr' = k^2$ by Corollary 10.3. Therefore A_1', ... , A_p' are spheres of radius r'. Meanwhile their points of contact lie on a circle a', of radius R' say, which is the image of the line a. Then $2RR' = k^2$ by Corollary 10.3. Therefore

$$\tan\left(\frac{180}{p}\right)^{\circ} = \frac{r'}{R'} = \frac{k^2/2r}{k^2/2R} = \frac{R}{r} = \cot\left(\frac{180}{q}\right)^{\circ}$$

$$\therefore \frac{180}{p} + \frac{180}{q} = 90.$$

$$\therefore \frac{1}{p} + \frac{1}{q} = \frac{1}{2}. \ \square$$

Corollary 12.2: The only examples of p, q are 3, 6 (or 6, 3) and 4, 4.

Proof:
$$2p + 2q = pq$$

$$\therefore pq - 2p - 2q + 4 = 4$$

$$\therefore (p - 2)(q - 2) = 4.$$

However, 4 can only factorise as 1×4, 2×2, 4×1; hence the three solutions. $\square$

Theorem 12.3: The 3, 6 interlock: given 4 spheres A_1, A_2, A_3, B_1 all touching one another then there is a 6-ring B_1, ... , B_6 interlocking the 3-ring A_1, A_2, A_3.

Proof: Invert in the point of contact of A_1, A_2. We obtain 2 parallel planes A_1', A_2' touching 2 equal touching spheres A_3', B_1'. There is a 6-ring B_1', ... , B_6' of equal spheres touching the 2 planes and surrounding and touching the sphere A_3'. The inverse image under the inversion gives the desired 6-ring. $\square$

Theorem 12.4: There exists a 4, 4 interlock.

Proof: Let $\alpha = (A_1, A_2, A_3, A_4)$ where A_1, A_2 are horizontal planes a distance $2r$ apart, and A_3, A_4 are equal spheres of radius $r/2$, one above the other, touching the planes.

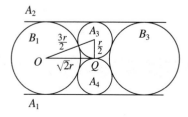

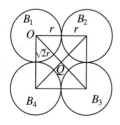

Let B_1 be a sphere of radius r, centre O say, touching A_1, A_2, A_3, A_4. Let Q be the point of contact of A_3A_4. Then $OQ = \sqrt{2}r$, by Pythagoras. Therefore OQ is half the diagonal of a square of side $2r$ and centre Q in a horizontal plane. Therefore the 4-ring $\beta = (B_1, B_2, B_3, B_4)$ of spheres of radius r and centred at the vertices of the square, interlocks α. Inverting in any point not on any of the spheres gives interlocking 4-rings of spheres. □

We now investigate the conditions that a 4-ring has to satisfy to be interlockable. Let α be a 4-ring, with the spheres not necessarily the same size, nor with their centres necessarily in a plane.

Theorem 12.5: The 4 points of contact lie on a circle, which we call the *contact* circle.

Proof: Invert in the point of contact of the first 2 spheres of the 4-ring α. These 2 spheres invert into horizontal planes A_1, A_2.

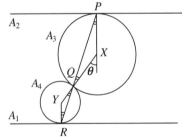

The other 2 spheres invert into spheres A_3, A_4 touching the planes and each other, but not necessarily of the same size, nor necessarily above one another. Let X, Y denote their centres, and let P, Q, R denote the points of contact between A_2 and A_3, A_3 and A_4, A_4 and A_1. The vertical plane containing X, Y also contains P, Q, R and the line XQY joining the centres. Let θ be the angle that this line makes with the vertical. Then by isosceles triangles

$$\angle PQX = \tfrac{1}{2}\theta = \angle RQY.$$

Therefore PQR is a straight line in the plane. Inverting back, the line PQR inverts into a circle through O containing all 4 points of contact of α. □

Theorem 12.6: A 4-ring is interlockable if and only if the contact circle is orthogonal to the 4 spheres, and the 4 contact points are harmonic.

Proof: Invert in the contact point of the first 2 spheres, giving 2 horizontal planes A_1, A_2 and 2 spheres A_3, A_4. There exists an interlocking ring if and only if these 2 spheres are the same size and one above the other. In other words the vertical contact line is orthogonal to the planes and spheres, and Q is the midpoint of PR. Inverting back preserves orthogonality by Theorem 10.4, and the harmonicity of the original points of contact by Theorem 11.4. □

13. Area of a sphere and volume of a ball

Since it is necessary to distinguish between the boundary and interior of a figure, we use the words circle, disc, sphere and ball as follows. The 1-dimensional *circle* is the boundary of the 2-dimensional *disc* inside, and the 2-dimensional *sphere* is the boundary surface of the solid 3-dimensional *ball* inside. We now give the original proofs of Archimedes (287-212 BC).

Theorem 13.1: The area of a sphere equals that of the enclosing cylinder.

Remark: This may well have been Archimedes' favourite theorem because the above diagram was inscribed on his tombstone in Syracuse in Sicily.

Proof: We show that corresponding thin slices of the sphere and cylinder between θ and $\theta + d\theta$ have equal areas.

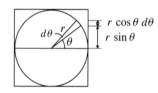

slice of	radius	length	width	$\therefore$ area
sphere	$r\cos\theta$	$2\pi r\cos\theta$	$r\,d\theta$	$2\pi r^2\cos\theta\,d\theta$
cylinder	r	$2\pi r$	$r\cos\theta\,d\theta$	$2\pi r^2\cos\theta\,d\theta$

Adding the slices (or integrating) gives the result. □

Corollary: The area of a sphere of radius r is $4\pi r^2$.

Proof: Area of sphere = area of cylinder
                          = circle × height
                          = $2\pi r \times 2r$
                          = $4\pi r^2$. □

Theorem 13.2: The volume of a ball of radius r is $\frac{4}{3}\pi r^3$.

Proof: In the proof Archimedes used the concept of balancing, which arose from his work in mechanics. Given a sphere of radius r, consider a cylinder of radius $2r$ and height $2r$, and a cone with the same base and height.

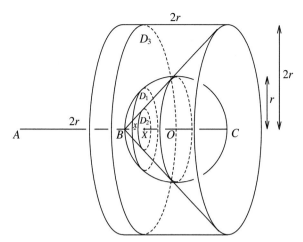

The cone and cylinder have axis BC, which is a horizontal diameter of the sphere. Let A be the point on BC extended, such that B is the midpoint of AC. Given a point X on BC, let $x = BX$, and let r_1, r_2, r_3 be the radii, and D_1, D_2, D_3 the areas, of the discs of intersection of the plane $\perp BC$ through X with the sphere, cone and cylinder. We claim that if D_1, D_2 are hung from A then they will balance D_3 at X with the fulcrum at B. For

$$r_1 = \sqrt{r^2 - (r - x)^2}, \text{ by Pythagoras}$$

$$= \sqrt{2rx - x^2}.$$

$$\therefore D_1 = \pi r_1^2 = \pi\left(2rx - x^2\right).$$

$$D_2 = \pi r_2^2 = \pi x^2, \text{ since } r_2 = x.$$

$$D_3 = \pi\left(2r\right)^2 = 4\pi r^2, \text{ since } r_3 = 2r.$$

$$\therefore 2r\left(D_1 + D_2\right) = 4\pi r^2 x = xD_3, \text{ giving the balance.}$$

Let V_1, V_2, V_3 denote the volumes of the sphere, cone and cylinder. Taking the union of the discs for all positions of X,

$$2r\left(V_1 + V_2\right) = rV_3.$$

since the centre of mass of the cylinder is the centre O of the sphere.

$$\therefore V_1 + V_2 = \tfrac{1}{2}V_3.$$

But $V_2 = \tfrac{1}{3}V_3$ by the Lemma below.

$$\therefore V_1 = \left(\tfrac{1}{2} - \tfrac{1}{3}\right)V_3 = \tfrac{1}{6}V_3 = \tfrac{1}{6}\pi\left(2r\right)^2 . 2r = \tfrac{4}{3}\pi r^3. \ \square$$

Lemma: The volume of the cone is a third the volume of the cylinder.
Proof: Let $d = 2r$. Then the circular cone V has height d and radius of base d. Let W be Dehn's pentahedron inscribed in a cube of edge d as

shown below (see Question 2.8). We can regard W as a square cone of height d on a square base of side d.

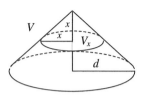
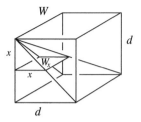

For $0 < x \leqslant d$ let V_x, W_x be horizontal sections of V, W at a vertical distance x below the vertices of the cones. Then V_x is a disc of radius x and area πx^2, while W_x is a square of side x and area x^2. Therefore the area $V_x = \pi W_x$. Therefore, combining all the sections, the volume $V = \pi W$. But $W = \frac{1}{3}d^3$ because 3 copies of W form the cube (see Question 2.9).

$$\therefore V = \tfrac{1}{3}\pi d^3 = \tfrac{1}{3}\left(\pi d^2\right)d = \tfrac{1}{3}\,(\text{volume of the cylinder}). \quad \square$$

14. Map projections

Definition: A *map projection* is a map from part of the surface of the Earth to a flat piece of paper.

However, it is impossible to map part of a sphere into a plane without some distortion. The map maker's choice of projection depends upon what the map is going to be used for. We shall consider 4 projections:

    (i)   Cylindrical projection

   (ii)   Mercator's projection

  (iii)   Central projection

  (iv)   Stereographic projection.

For coordinates on the Earth we use latitude θ and longitude ϕ.

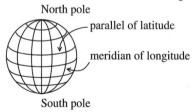

Definitions: The *circles of latitude*, given by $\theta = $ constant, $-\pi/2 \leqslant \theta \leqslant \pi/2$, are horizontal circles running from $\theta = -\pi/2$ at the south pole to $\theta = \pi/2$ at the north pole. The *meridians of longitude*, given by $\phi = $ constant, $0 \leqslant \phi < 2\pi$, are halves of great circles, each joining the North pole to the South pole.

(i) *Cylindrical projection*

Definition: Use Archimedes' tombstone diagram (see the last section) to project the Earth horizontally onto the enclosing cylinder, cut the cylinder open along a meridian, unroll it flat, and scale down to the size of the paper.

This has the advantage of mapping latitude and longitude onto a rectangular grid. Also by Archimedes' Theorem 13.1 it preserves areas, that is mapping equal areas on the sphere to equal areas on the paper. But it suffers from the disadvantage of not being conformal, and hence distorts all shapes, especially those far from the Equator.

Theorem 14.1: In the cylindrical projection a small square at latitude θ is mapped to a rectangle, expanded horizontally by $\sec\theta$ and shrunk vertically by $\cos\theta$. Hence a small circle is mapped to an ellipse, whose ratio of major axis to minor axis is $\sec^2\theta$.

Proof: The point (ϕ, θ) on the sphere is mapped to $(r\phi, r\sin\theta)$ on the cylinder. The small rectangle at (ϕ, θ) induced by the small increments $(d\phi, d\theta)$ has sides $(r\cos\theta\, d\phi, r\, d\theta)$, and is mapped to the small rectangle

$$\left(r\, d\phi,\ d\left(r\sin\theta\right)\right) \ = \ \left(r\, d\phi,\ r\cos\theta\, d\theta\right).$$

Therefore the horizontal sides are expanded by $\sec\theta$, and the vertical sides shrunk by $\cos\theta$. Therefore the ratio of major axis to minor axis of the ellipse is $\sec^2\theta$. Consequently, the direction NW is crushed down towards W, and so the angle of $45°$ between N and NW is expanded to nearly $90°$, illustrating its non-conformality. □

(ii) *Mercator's projection*

Gerhard Kremer (1512-1594), known as Mercator, invented a conformal modification of the cylindrical projection as follows.

Definition: Define *Mercator's projection* by suitably stretching the vertical latitude axis of the cylindrical projection to make it conformal.

Theorem 14.2: Mercator's projection maps $(\phi, \theta) \to (\phi, \log(\sec\theta + \tan\theta))$.

Proof: Suppose $(\phi, \theta) \to (\phi, f(\theta))$.   The small square with sides $(r\cos\theta\, d\phi, r\, d\theta)$ is mapped to the square $(r\, d\phi, rf'(\theta)\, d\theta)$. The horizontal expansion is $\sec\theta$, and by conformality the vertical expansion must be the same.

$$\therefore f(\theta) \ = \ \int \sec\theta\, d\theta \ = \ \log\left(\sec\theta + \tan\theta\right) + c.$$

But $f(0) \ = \ 0$ by choice and so $c \ = \ 0$. □

I used to be a navigator in the air force during World War II, and navigators like Mercator's projection because, being conformal, it preserves angles. Therefore straight lines on the map represent paths on the globe resulting from steering a fixed course, with a fixed compass setting. Also small islands are shown with the correct shape, which aids map reading. A disadvantage of Mercator's projection is that it tends to infinity at the poles. Hence equal areas at different latitudes on the earth do not get mapped to equal areas on the map.

(iii) *Central projection*

Definition: Let T be the tangent plane at the south pole S. Define *central projection* by projecting the southern hemisphere radially from the centre O onto T.

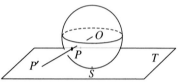

It maps the southern circles of latitude to concentric circles, centre S, and meridians of longitude to rays emanating from S. Central projection has the advantage of mapping great circles on the sphere to straight lines on the map, because a great circle is the intersection of the sphere with a plane through O. Hence the shortest path between two points on the sphere is accurately represented by the straight line between their images on the map.

The disadvantages are that it is not conformal, and as points approach the equator their images tend to infinity. However, the projection is relatively accurate near the south pole. Similarly central projection onto the tangent plane at any other point on the sphere is relatively accurate near that point.

(iv) *Stereographic projection*

Definition: Again let T be the tangent plane at the south pole S. Define *stereographic projection* by projecting the sphere Σ minus the north pole N radially from N onto T.

Like central projection, it maps circles of latitude to concentric circles, centre S, and meridians of longitude to rays emanating from S.

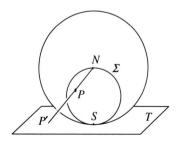

Theorem 14.3: Stereographic projection is conformal. It maps circles in Σ through N to lines in T, and circles in Σ not through N to circles in T.

Proof: Let f be inversion in the sphere centre N and radius NS. By Theorem 10.1(iii) f maps $\Sigma - N$ radially from N to T, and therefore $f \mid \Sigma - N$ is the same as stereographic projection. By Theorem 10.4 f is conformal. By Corollary 10.2 f maps circles through N to lines, and circles not through N to circles. $\square$

The conformality, implying preservation of angles, makes stereographic projection navigationally desirable. It also maps the whole sphere except for the north pole, but as points approach the north pole their images tend to infinity. It is relatively accurate near the south pole. Similarly the sphere can be stereographically projected onto any tangent plane. For further reading see George Jennings [12, pp. 63-82].

15. Knotting

Topology is sometimes called 'rubber-sheet' geometry because it studies properties like knotting and linking, which are much deeper than those in previous sections because they persist under much more general rubber-like transformations (homeomorphisms). Consequently the style of proof will be quite different.

knotting   linking

Definitions: A *knot* is a closed curve in $\mathbb{R}^3$. Two knots are *equal* if one can be moved into the other.

Example 1:

trefoil

Proof:

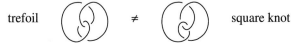

$\square$

Definition: Two knots are *unequal* if one cannot be moved into the other.

Example 2:

trefoil $\qquad$ $\neq$ $\qquad$ square knot

Definition: A curve is *knotted* if it is unequal to a circle.

To prove equality between 2 knots (or unknottedness) we have to demonstrate it geometrically, as in the example above, whereas to prove inequality between 2 knots (or knottedness) we have to do it algebraically by introducing an *invariant*, in other words a property that does not vary if the knot is moved, proving that it is invariant, and verifying that the two knots have different values of the invariant.

Let *K* be a picture of a knot, with a finite number of crossings. At each crossing the *underpass* is indicated by a break in the curve, and so the curve is broken into a finite number of arcs.

Definition: We say *K* can be *3-coloured* if the following holds. Each arc is one colour, and

(1) at least 2 of the 3 colours are used;

(2) at each crossing 1 or 3 colours are used

(for the overpass and the 2 sides of the underpass).

In our drawings we shall use for the three colours continuous curves, dashed curves and dotted curves.

Lemma 1: The trefoil can be 3-coloured.

Proof:

   □

Lemma 2: The circle cannot be 3-coloured.

Proof: Being all one colour it would violate condition (1).   □

Theorem 15.1: 3-colourability is an invariant.

Proof: We have to show that if *K* can be 3-coloured, and *K* is moved to *L*, then *L* can be 3-coloured. Consider the following 5 types of elementary move:

Type I (and its inverse)

Type II (and its inverse)

Type III (which can be seen to equal its own inverse by turning the paper upside down).

$$-\!\!\bigwedge\!\!- \longrightarrow \overline{}\!\!\bigvee\!\!-$$

If $K \rightarrow L$ is a long complicated move imagine taking a film of it and examining the film frame by frame. At each frame there is either no change in the configuration of arcs from the previous frame, or else there has been one of the 5 types of elementary move shown above. Therefore we can interpret the complicated move $K \rightarrow L$ as a finite sequence of elementary moves. For instance, in the proof of the Example 1 above, the first and last steps represent no change in the configuration, while the second and third steps are elementary moves of types III and I.

If we prove the theorem for elementary moves then it follows for any sequence of such, and hence for any move. In each case we are given a 3-colouring before the elementary move, and have to show there is a 3-colouring after the elementary move, without changing the colouring of the rest of the knot, or of the ends of the arcs in the elementary move that are attached to the rest of the knot.

Type I (and its inverse):

$$\mathcal{R} \longleftrightarrow \frown$$

Type II (and its inverse): there are 2 cases depending on whether the ends are coloured the same or different.

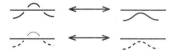

Type III: there are 5 cases, and in each case we have to show that it is possible to achieve a colouring satisfying condition (2) by recolouring the little arc in the middle without changing the colours of the other arcs, since they are all attached to the rest of the knot.

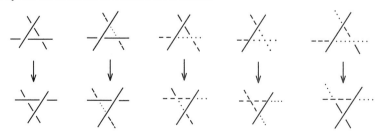

This completes the proof of Theorem 15.1. $\square$

Corollary: The trefoil is knotted.

Proof: Otherwise the unknotting would move the trefoil into a circle, violating the invariance of 3-colourability. □

Lemma: The square knot cannot be 3-coloured.

Proof: The square knot contains 4 arcs, and therefore in any attempted 3-colouring 2 of them must be the same colour. But any 2 arcs meet at some crossing. Therefore the overpass at this crossing must be the same colour by condition (2). Similarly the fourth arc must also be the same colour, violating condition (1). □

Corollary: Trefoil ≠ square knot.

Proof: One can be 3-coloured and the other cannot be. □

However, this invariant is no good for proving that the square knot is knotted, because neither the square knot nor the circle can be 3-coloured. Therefore we need to generalise the invariant, and for this we shall use arithmetic modulo p, as follows.

Definition of mod p arithmetic: Let p be an odd prime. The *integers modulo p* consist of the set 0, 1, 2, ... , $p - 1$. Given two integers a, b we write $a = b \pmod{p}$ if they differ by a multiple of p.

Definition: We say a knot K has *code p* if the arcs can be labelled with integers modulo p such that

(1) at least 2 arcs are labelled differently, and

(2) at each crossing the average of the two underpasses equals the overpass $(\text{mod } p)$:

$$a + b = 2c \pmod{p}.$$

We leave it to the reader to verify that a knot has code 3 if and only if it can be 3-coloured (see Question 15.1).   Hence the codes are indeed a generalisation of 3-colouring.

Lemma: The square knot has code 5.

Proof: Check each crossing going round the knot:

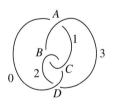

A	$1 + 0 = 6 \pmod 5$
B	$3 + 1 = 4$
C	$0 + 2 = 2$
D	$2 + 3 = 0 \pmod 5$. □

Theorem 15.2: Codes are invariant.

Proof: It suffices to check the elementary moves.

Type I (and its inverse)

Type II (and its inverse)

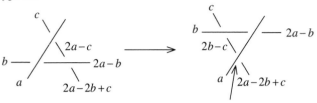

Type III

Check: $(2b - c) + (2a - 2b + c) = 2a$.

This completes the proof of Theorem 15.2. □

Corollary: The square knot is knotted.
Proof: The circle has no codes, otherwise condition (1) would be violated. □

Definition: The *reflection* of a knot is given by changing each crossing.

Some knots, like the trefoil, are unequal to their reflection. Others, like the square knot, are equal to their reflection (see Question 15.5).

Definition: The *product* of 2 knots is given by cutting and joining them together.

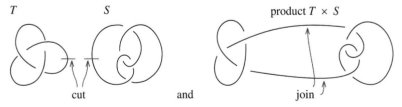

In Question 15.2 we show that the codes of $T \times S$ are those of T and S.

Definition: A knot is called *prime* if it is not the product of two (simpler) knots.

The list of all 14 prime knots with fewer than 8 crossings is shown below, together with their codes. More precisely, if a prime knot has less than 8 crossings then it, or its reflection, equals one of those on the list. Since the circle has no codes this proves that they are all knotted. It does not prove, however, that those with the same code are unequal, and that requires a more sophisticated invariant (see Raymond Lickorish [14]). Notice that two of the knots in the list have more than one code.

List of all prime knots with fewer than 8 crossings

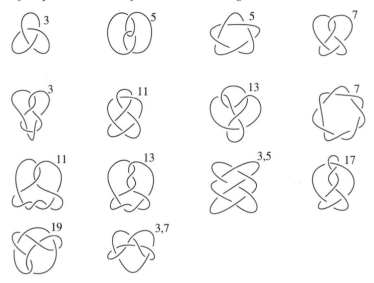

16. Linking

Linking is one of the most characteristic features of 3 dimensions. It is intuitively and experimentally obvious that linked curves cannot be separated, but we shall prove this mathematically by constructing an invariant called the *linking number L* that measures how many times one curve links the other.

$$L = 0 \qquad L = 1 \qquad L = 2 \qquad L = 0 \qquad L = 1$$

Incidentally the same proof can be used to show that two spheres can be linked in 5-dimensions, where intuition is less obvious and experiment is impossible.

Definitions: To *orient* a curve means to choose one or other of the two directions going round the curve; the orientation is indicated by an arrow. To *span* a curve means to choose a disc whose boundary is the curve. The disc itself may be curved, and may intersect itself if the curve happens to be knotted.

Definition of linking number L: Given two curves A, B choose:

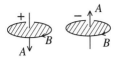

(i)   orientations of A and B;
(ii) either A or B to span, say B; and
(iii) a disc b spanning B.

Then A will pierce b in a finite number of points.

We call a particular piercing *positive* if A pierces b in the direction that a right-handed corkscrew would move if it were screwed in the direction of the orientation of B; otherwise call it *negative*. Let P be the number of positive piercings and N the number of negative piercings. Define the *linking number L* to be the absolute difference between P and N.

Example

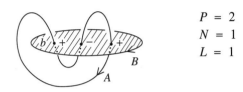

P = 2
N = 1
L = 1

Theorem 16: L is invariant.

Proof: We have to prove firstly that L is independent of the 3 choices, and secondly that it does not vary when the curves are moved. The second part is easy because if the disc is moved along with the curves then the number of piercings will be conserved. Hence the burden of proof lies in showing that L is independent of the 3 choices.

(i)   If one of the orientations is reversed then the sign of each piercing is reversed. Therefore P and N are interchanged, and their difference L is the same.

(ii) Suppose we chose to span A rather than B, and chose a disc a spanning A. Let P' and N' be the numbers of positive and negative piercings of a by B, and let L' be their difference. We have to show that L = L'.

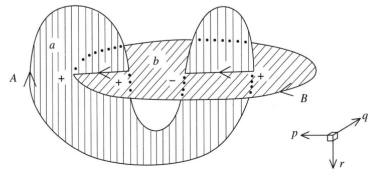

By moving a into general position relative to b if necessary then the intersection of a and b will consist of a finite number of arcs and closed curves. (If a is *not* in general position relative to b, then their intersection might include some 2-dimensional regions, but an arbitrarily small perturbation of a will bring it into general position and cure that defect, making the intersection 1-dimensional.) Forget the closed curves and concentrate on the arcs because their ends will be the piercings of b by A and a by B. Orient the arcs so that at each point, if **p** is a vector giving the orientation of the arc, and **q**, **r** are vectors giving positive piercing of a, b, then (**p**, **q**, **r**) is a right-handed set of axes. Then the front ends of the arcs will be the positive piercings of a by B and the negative piercings of b by A, while the back ends will be the complementary piercings. But the number of front ends is the same as the number of back ends. Therefore $P' + N = N' + P$.   Therefore $P - N = P' - N'$. Therefore $L = L'$, as required.

(iii) Finally suppose we chose a different disc b'' spanning B, giving rise to a linking number L''. Then $L'' = L' = L$ by (ii) above, and so $L'' = L$, as required. $\square$

Codes of links: One can define codes for links exactly as for knots. The definition is the same, and the invariance theorem 15.1 is the same.

Examples:

all codes   no codes

On the whole, in linking theory, codes are less useful than linking numbers. However, when given curves for which $L = 0$, then codes may be useful in showing that they are, nevertheless, linked. (See Questions 16.3 and 16.4.)

Remark: At first sight knotting and linking seem somewhat similar, but in fact they are quite different phenomena, as can be seen in higher dimensions. Knotting is a codimension 2 problem, while linking is a $(2n + 1)$-dimensional problem. For instance a sphere can be knotted in 4 dimensions [2] but unknotted in 5 dimensions [18], whereas two spheres can be linked in 5 dimensions. Similarly a 50-dimensional sphere can be knotted in 52 dimensions but unknotted in 53 dimensions, whereas two 50-dimensional spheres can be linked in 101 dimensions.

Further reading: I have found the following books very accessible and helpful on many of the topics: Coxeter [6], Courant and Robbins [4], Hilbert and Cohn-Vossen [11], and Jennings [12].

APPENDIX 1: Exercises

1. Spherical triangles

Question 1.1

Find the angles and area of a face of a spherical equilateral tetrahedron.

Verify that they satisfy Theorem 1.

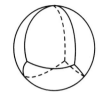

2. Angles in a tetrahedron

Question 2.1

Show that in an equilateral tetrahedron each edge angle is $\sec^{-1} 3$, and each solid angle is $\frac{3}{2} \sec^{-1} 3 - \frac{1}{4}$.

Remark: In this and the following question, the inverse trigonometrical functions are to be evaluated in edge-angle units.

Question 2.2

A unit right-angled tetrahedron is defined by taking a unit distance along three perpendicular axes. Show that

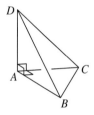

$$\text{edge-angles at} \begin{cases} AB, AC, AD &= \frac{1}{4} \\ BC, CD, DB &= \tan^{-1}\sqrt{2} \end{cases}$$

$$\text{solid-angles at} \begin{cases} A &= \frac{1}{8} \\ B, C, D &= \tan^{-1}\sqrt{2} - \frac{1}{8}. \end{cases}$$

Question 2.3

Dehn's tetrahedron is defined in a cube as shown. Prove that

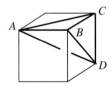

$$\text{edge-angles at} \begin{cases} AB, CD &= \frac{1}{8} \\ AC, BC, BD &= \frac{1}{4} \\ AD &= \frac{1}{6} \end{cases}$$

$$\text{solid-angles at} \begin{cases} A, D &= \frac{1}{48} \\ B, C &= \frac{1}{16.} \end{cases}$$

Question 2.4

Make Dehn's tetrahedron by drawing the net below on thin cardboard, cutting out, scoring along the internal edges, folding them down, and taping together the other edges.

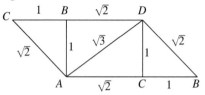

Question 2.5

Make a mirror image of Dehn's tetrahedron by using the same net, but folding the internal edges up (instead of down) before taping them together.

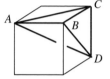

Question 2.6

Show that the plane bisecting and perpendicular the diagonal *AD* of a cube meets the 6 faces in a regular hexagon.

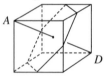

Question 2.7

Make 3 copies of Dehn's tetrahedron and 3 copies of its mirror image; fit them together to form a cube, holding them together with an elastic band round the hexagon of Question 2.6.

Question 2.8

Make Dehn's pentahedron, the union of his tetrahedron and its mirror image, from the following net.

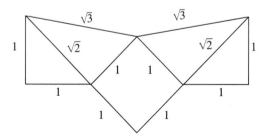

Question 2.9

Make 3 copies of Dehn's pentahedron, and show they fit together to form a cube, held together by an elastic band as in Question 2.7.

Question 2.10

Show that 4 unit right-angled tetrahedra and an equilateral tetrahedron of edge $\sqrt{2}$ fit together to form a cube. Verify that the edge and solid angles add correctly.

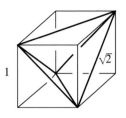

3.   *Concurrencies in a tetrahedron*

Question 3.1

Show that the centre of mass G of a tetrahedron $ABCD$ is the midpoint of each of the joins of midpoints of opposite edges.

Question 3.2

In a tetrahedron $\Delta = ABCD$ define the *face-trisector* of ABC to be the line through the circumcentre of, and $\perp$ to, ABC; it is the line of points equidistant from A, B, C. Show that the 4 face-trisectors meet at the circumcentre S of Δ.

Question 3.3

In a tetrahedron $\Delta = ABCD$ define the *vertex-trisector* of A to be the line of points equidistant from the faces b, c, d. Show that the 4 vertex-trisectors meet at the incentre I of Δ.

Question 3.4

Show that if 2 pairs of opposite edges of a tetrahedron are $\perp$ then the third pair is also.

Question 3.5

Show that if the opposite edges of a tetrahedron are $\perp$ then the foot of each altitude of the tetrahedron is the orthocentre of the opposite face.

Question 3.6

Show that in a tetrahedron $ABCD$ if the altitude through A is the orthocentre of BCD then the opposite edges of $ABCD$ are $\perp$.

Question 3.7

Given BCD, show that $ABCD$ has opposite edges $\perp$ if and only if A lies on the line through the orthocentre of, and $\perp$ to, BCD. Deduce that, given BCD, there are ∞ positions of A for which the altitudes meet, but ∞^3 positions of A for which they do meet.

4. Perspective

Question 4.1

Let E be the eye, and X, Y, Z the 3 vanishing points for a cube. Let H be the foot of the $\perp$ from E onto XYZ. Show that H is the orthocentre of XYZ.

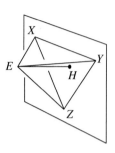

Question 4.2

Show that if X, Y, Z are the vanishing points for a cube then XYZ is an acute-angled triangle.

Question 4.3

With the notation of Question 4.1, show that if XYZ is an equilateral triangle of side 1 then $EH = 1/\sqrt{6}$.

Question 4.4

The diagram shows a perspective drawing of a cube with vanishing points X, Y, Z and H the orthocentre of XYZ.

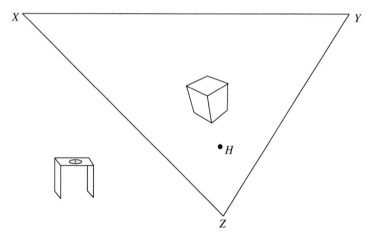

Cut out a cardboard shape as shown below, punch a hole, and bend along the lines to form a peephole. Place the peephole over H and with the eye at the peephole confirm that the cube looks cubical.

Question 4.5

Using the same peephole as in the last question, placed over *H*, confirm that all the cubes look cubical, of the same size, and with parallel faces.

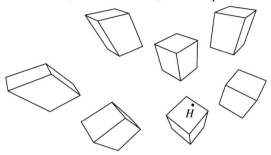

Question 4.6

The following perspective drawing of a cube uses two vanishing points *X*, *Y* for 8 of the edges, where *XY* is horizontal, and has the other 4 edges drawn vertical (in effect *Z* has descended to minus infinity). Prove that the drawing will look like a cuboid whenever the eye is placed on the horizontal semicircle with diameter *XY*. Confirm this experimentally by placing the eye near *X* and rotating the paper so as to slide the eye round the semicircle to *Y*. Watch the box changing from a matchbox shape when the eye begins near *X* to a cube when the eye is in front of *C*.

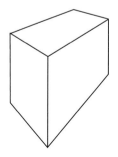

5. *Desargues' theorem*

Question 5.1

Suppose triangles *T*, *T′* are coplanar. Use the 3-dimensional Theorem 5 to show that they are in point perspective if and only if they are in line perspective.

Question 5.2

Suppose triangles T, T' are coplanar. Without appealing to the 3-dimensional Theorem 5 use projective coordinates to show that if they are in point perspective then they are in line perspective.

6.   *Regular polyhedra*

Question 6.1

List the numbers of faces, edges and vertices of each of the 5 regular polyhedra, and verify that each satisfies Euler's formula.

Question 6.2

Make the 5 regular polyhedra.

Question 6.3

Let c, m, i denote the diameters of the circumsphere, midsphere and insphere of a regular polyhedron of edge 1. Prove that $c^2 = m^2 + 1$, and that if the polyhedron has triangular faces then $i^2 = m^2 - \frac{1}{3}$.

Question 6.4

Prove that the diameters of the 3 spheres associated with each of the regular tetrahedron and octahedron are as in Theorem 6.2.

Question 6.5

Show that in a regular pentagon of edge 1 the diagonal g is the positive solution of $g^2 - g - 1 = 0$, namely $g = (1 + \sqrt{5})/2$.

Remark: Kepler called g the *golden ratio*. He called it a *ratio* because it is the ratio of diagonal to edge in any regular pentagon. It was originally introduced by Euclid in [8, Book VI, Definition 3]. He defined a line to have been *cut in extreme and mean ratio* when, as the whole line is to the greater segment, so is the greater to the less. In other words if $a > b$ are the lengths of the two segments into which the line has been cut then

$$(a + b)/a = a/b \qquad \therefore ab + b^2 = a^2$$
$$\therefore (a/b)^2 - a/b - 1 = 0 \qquad \therefore a/b = g.$$

Question 6.6

Show that the diameters of the incircle and circumcircle of a regular pentagon of edge 1 are $\sqrt{1 + 2/\sqrt{5}}$ and $\sqrt{2 + 2/\sqrt{5}}$.

Question 6.7

Show that a regular icosahedron of edge 1 can be embedded in a cube of edge g (the golden ratio), so that each face of the cube contains an edge of the icosahedron. Deduce the diameters of the 3 spheres associated with the icosahedron, as in Theorem 6.2.

Question 6.8

Prove that a cube of edge g (the golden ratio) can be embedded in a regular dodecahedron of edge 1, so that each vertex of the cube is a vertex of the dodecahedron. Show that there are 5 such cubes. Deduce the diameters of the 3 spheres associated with the dodecahedron, as in Theorem 6.2.

Question 6.9

Make a stella octangula, which is the non-convex union of dual tetrahedra. List the numbers of faces, edges and vertices, and verify that they satisfy Euler's formula.

Question 6.10

Restricting the faces to triangles, squares, pentagons and hexagons, prove there are exactly 15 semi-regular polyhedra. List the vertex patterns and the numbers of faces, edges and vertices, and verify that they satisfy Euler's formula.

Question 6.11

Make the 15 semi-regular polyhedra. Note that the midedge dodecahedron, buckminsterfullerene, and the snub cube and snub dodecahedron are particularly beautiful.

Question 6.12

Make a rhombic dodecahedron from the following net.

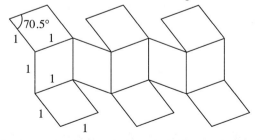

Question 6.13

Verify that the rhombic dodecahedron satisfies Euler's formula.

7. *Rotation groups*

Question 7.1
Show that D_n is the rotation group of the n-prism ($n \neq 4$) and the n-antiprism ($n \neq 3$). Explain why there are the 2 exceptions.

Question 7.2
Show that D_4 is the rotation group of the twisted mitred cube.

Question 7.3
Write out the 12×12 multiplication table for A_4. Hint: put the identity first, then the (2,2)-cycles and finally the 3-cycles.

Question 7.4
Show that the *mitred tetrahedron*, defined by replacing each vertex of the tetrahedron by a triangle, each edge by a square and each face by a smaller triangle, is the same as the midedge cube. Explain why its rotation group is S_4 rather than A_4 inherited from the tetrahedron.

Question 7.5
Show that the rotation group of a rhombus is D_2. Write out the multiplication table and verify that it is abelian.

8. *Tessellations and sphere packings*

Question 8.1
Show there is a tessellation of $\mathbb{R}^3$ using Dehn's tetrahedron and its mirror image in equal numbers.

Question 8.2
Show there is a tessellation of $\mathbb{R}^3$ using Dehn's pentahedron (see Question 2.8).

Question 8.3
Show there is a tessellation of $\mathbb{R}^3$ using right-angled tetrahedra and regular tetrahedra of edge $\sqrt{2}$, in the ratio of 4:1.

Question 8.4
Show there is a tessellation of $\mathbb{R}^3$ using regular tetrahedra and octagons in the ratio of 2:1.

Question 8.5
How many spheres are there in a tetrahedron of spheres, of edge length 4 spheres, built according to the barrow boy's packing? Make such a tetrahedron with marbles and glass-to-glass superglue.

Question 8.6
Let A denote the square packing of spheres and B the barrow boy's packing. Show that (in a large region) the ratio of the number of spheres in a layer of A to that of B is $\sqrt{3}/2$, and that the ratio of the number of layers of A to that of B is $2/\sqrt{3}$. Hence the number of spheres in both packings is the same, confirming Theorem 8.2.

Question 8.7
Make a rhombic-trapezoid dodecahedron from the following net.

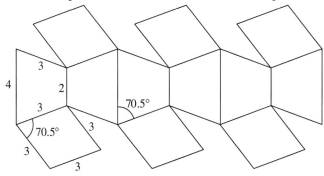

Question 8.8
Verify that the rhombic-trapezoid dodecahedron has the same numbers of faces, edges and vertices as the rhombic dodecahedron. Describe the vertex patterns, and identify its rotation group.

Question 8.9
Show that the cells of the tessellation of $\mathbb{R}^3$ induced by the hexagonal sphere packing are rhombic-trapezoid dodecahedra.

9.   *Conics*

Question 9.1

Draw an ellipse by moving a pencil X inside a loop of cotton held taut around two drawing pins F, F'. By changing the length of the loop draw a family of ellipses, the larger the more circular, and the smaller the flatter with greater eccentricity.

Question 9.2

Show that if $\alpha > \beta$ the conic is a hyperbola. (Here, and in Question 9.4, α and β are defined on page 26.)

Question 9.3

Show that, in a suitable coordinate system, the equation of a hyperbola is
$$\left(\frac{x}{a}\right)^2 - \left(\frac{y}{b}\right)^2 = 1.$$

Question 9.4

Show that if $\alpha = \beta$ the conic is a parabola.

Question 9.5

Show that, in a suitable coordinate system, the equation of a parabola is $y^2 = 4ax$.

Question 9.6

Explain why a circle looks elliptical when viewed from a point off its axis.

Question 9.7

Describe the shape of a crescent moon.

10. *Inversion*

Question 10.1

Show that the angle between a chord and a tangent of a circle equals the angle subtended by the chord in the opposite segment of the circle.

Question 10.2

Show that inversion does not preserve the centres of spheres or circles.

11. *Cross ratios*

Question 11.1

Show that in a complete quadrilateral the diagonal vertices separate harmonically the quadrilateral vertices: $(APBQ) = -1$.

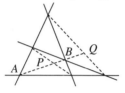

12. *Rings of spheres*

Question 12.1

Show that in general a tetrahedron has no midsphere touching all the edges

Question 12.2

Prove that the following 3 conditions on a tetrahedron are equivalent:

 (i) The 3 sums of opposite edges are equal.
 (ii) There exists a midsphere touching all the edges.
 (iii) There are 4 spheres centred at the 4 vertices all touching one another.

Show that the 6 points of contact of the 4 spheres are the points where the midsphere touches the 6 edges.

Question 12.3

Show that if a 4-ring of spheres is interlockable then the centres of the spheres lie in a plane. Show, further, that if two 4-rings interlock then their planes are ⊥.

13. *Areas of spheres and volumes of balls*

Question 13.1

Prove, using calculus, that the volume of a cone on any shaped base equals $\frac{1}{3}$ base × height .

Question 13.2

Prove, using calculus, that the volume of a sphere of radius r equals $\frac{4}{3}\pi r^3$.

14. *Map projections*

Question 14.1

Show that central projection has ratio of vertical expansion to horizontal expansion equal to cosec θ at latitude $-\theta$, and is therefore not conformal.

Question 14.2

Show that stereographic projection has equal horizontal and vertical expansions at latitude θ, confirming that it is conformal.

15. *Knotting*

Question 15.1

Show that codes are a generalisation of 3-colouring.

Question 15.2

Show that the product of the trefoil and the square knot has codes 3 and 5.

Question 15.3

Prove that the codes of all the prime knots with fewer than 8 crossings are as shown in the diagram at the end of Section 15.

Question 15.4

Prove that any knot has only a finite number of codes.

Question 15.5

Show that the square knot is equal to its reflection.

16. *Linking*

Question 16.1

Show that 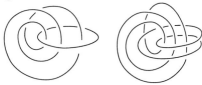 has $L = 2$. Is it equal to ?

Question 16.2

Calculate the linking numbers of

Question 16.3

Show that Whitehead's link below has $L = 0$. This does not imply, however, that the 2 curves are unlinked. Prove that they are in fact linked by showing that Whitehead's link does not have code 3, but a pair of unlinked curves does.

Question 16.4

Draw an example of 3 linked curves that are pairwise unlinked, and prove that they are linked.

APPENDIX 2: Solutions

1. *Spherical triangles*

Solution 1.1

Angle = $\frac{1}{3}(360°)$ = 120°.   Area = $\frac{1}{4}S$.

$$A + B + C = 360 = 180\left(1 + 4\left(\frac{\frac{1}{4}S}{S}\right)\right). \quad \square$$

2. *Angles in a tetrahedron*

Solution 2.1

Suppose the edges of the tetrahedron are of length 1.

By symmetry all the edge-angles are equal, and all the solid-angles are equal. Let E be the midpoint of AB.

By Pythagoras $CE = DE = \sqrt{3}/2$.

Let θ = edge-angle of $AB = \angle CED$.

From the cosine formula for triangle CDE,

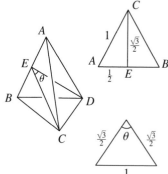

$$1 = \tfrac{3}{4} + \tfrac{3}{4} - 2.\tfrac{3}{4}.\cos\theta$$

$$\therefore \tfrac{3}{2}\cos\theta = \tfrac{1}{2} \therefore \cos\theta = \tfrac{1}{3} \therefore \theta = \cos^{-1}\tfrac{1}{3} = \sec^{-1}3 = 70.53...°$$

$$\therefore \text{ in edge-angle units } \theta = \sec^{-1}3 = \tfrac{70.53}{360} = 0.1959... .$$

By Theorem 2, solid-angle = $\frac{1}{4}\left(6\sec^{-1}3 - 1\right) = \frac{3}{2}\sec^{-1}3 - \frac{1}{4} = 0.0439... .$ $\square$

Solution 2.2

The faces meeting along the edges AB, AC, AD are $\perp$ and so their edge-angles are each $\frac{1}{4}$. Let E be the midpoint of BC. By Pythagoras $AE = 1/\sqrt{2}$.

Let $\theta = \angle AED$ = edge-angles at BC, CD, DB.

Then $\tan\theta = \sqrt{2}. \therefore \theta = \tan^{-1}\sqrt{2} = 54.74...°.$

$\therefore$ in edge-angle units $\theta = \tan^{-1}\sqrt{2} = \frac{54.74}{360} = 0.1520... .$

Solid-angle at $A = \frac{1}{8}$, since there are 8 quadrants.

Let ψ = solid-angle at B, C, D. Then by Theorem 2,

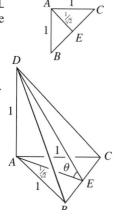

$$\tfrac{1}{8} + 3\psi = \tfrac{3}{4} + 3\tan^{-1}\sqrt{2} - 1$$

$$\therefore 3\psi = 3\tan^{-1}\sqrt{2} - \tfrac{3}{8}$$

$$\therefore \psi = \tan^{-1}\sqrt{2} - \tfrac{1}{8} = 0.0270... . \quad \square$$

Solution 2.3

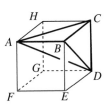

In Dehn's tetrahedron the faces containing AB meet at 45°, and so the edge-angle $= \frac{1}{8}$. Similarly for CD. The faces containing BC meet at 90°, and so the edge-angle $= \frac{1}{4}$. Similarly for AC, BD. One can fill the cube with 6 Dehn's tetrahedra (3 of which are mirror images) $ABCD$, $ABED$, $AFED$, $AFGD$, $AHGD$, $AHCD$. (See also Question 2.7.) Each of these has the same edge-angle at AD, and they sum to 1. Therefore the edge-angle at AD is $\frac{1}{6}$. The solid-angles of the 6 tetrahedra at A sum to the solid-angle of a cube which is $\frac{1}{8}$. Therefore the solid-angle at A is $\frac{1}{48}$. Similarly at D. The solid-angles at B of the 2 tetrahedra with a vertex at B sum to $\frac{1}{8}$, and hence each is $\frac{1}{16}$. Similarly at C.

Check Theorem 2:

$$\frac{2}{48} + \frac{2}{16} = \frac{2}{8} + \frac{3}{4} + \frac{1}{6} - 1. \;\;\square$$

Solution 2.6

The midpoints of the 6 edges of the cube not containing A, D are equidistant from A, D. Therefore so are their 6 joins on the 6 faces of the cube, which together form a hexagon in the plane bisecting AD. By symmetry, it is regular. $\square$

Solution 2.10

Let $\theta = \sec^{-1} 3$, $\psi = \tan^{-1} \sqrt{2}$.

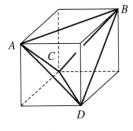

Lemma: $\theta + 2\psi = \frac{1}{2}$ (in edge-angle units).

Proof:

$$2 \cos^2 \tfrac{1}{2}\theta - 1 = \tfrac{1}{3}$$

$$\therefore \cos^2 \tfrac{1}{2}\theta = \tfrac{2}{3} \quad \therefore \cos \tfrac{1}{2}\theta = \sqrt{\tfrac{2}{3}}$$

$$\psi = \tan^{-1}\sqrt{2} = \sin^{-1}\sqrt{\tfrac{2}{3}}$$

$$\therefore \tfrac{1}{2}\theta + \psi = 90° \quad \therefore \theta + 2\psi = \tfrac{1}{2} \text{ (in edge-angle units). } \square$$

$$
\begin{aligned}
\text{Solid-angle at } A &= \left(\tfrac{3}{2}\sec^{-1}3 - \tfrac{1}{4}\right) + 3\left(\tan^{-1}\sqrt{2} - \tfrac{1}{8}\right)\\
&= \tfrac{3}{2}\theta - \tfrac{1}{4} + 3\psi - \tfrac{3}{8}\\
&= \tfrac{3}{2}(\theta + 2\psi) - \tfrac{5}{8}\\
&= \tfrac{3}{4} - \tfrac{5}{8}, \text{ by the Lemma}\\
&= \tfrac{1}{8} = \text{solid-angle of the cube}
\end{aligned}
$$

$$
\begin{aligned}
\text{Edge-angle at } AB &= \sec^{-1}3 + 2\tan^{-1}\sqrt{2}\\
&= \tfrac{1}{2}, \text{ by the Lemma}\\
&= \text{edge-angle at a face of the cube. } \square
\end{aligned}
$$

3. *Concurrencies in a tetrahedron*

Solution 3.1

$$\mathbf{g} = \frac{1}{2}\left(\frac{\mathbf{a} + \mathbf{b}}{2} + \frac{\mathbf{c} + \mathbf{d}}{2}\right). \ \square$$

Solution 3.2

S lies on the face-trisector of ABC because $SA = SB = SC$. Similarly, S lies on the other face-trisectors. $\square$

Solution 3.3

I lies on the vertex-trisector of A because it is equidistant from b, c, d. Similarly for the other vertex-trisectors. $\square$

Solution 3.4

Let $\mathbf{a}$, $\mathbf{b}$, $\mathbf{c}$, $\mathbf{d}$ denote the coordinates of the vertices A, B, C, D.

$$AB \perp CD \implies (\mathbf{a} - \mathbf{b}).(\mathbf{c} - \mathbf{d}) = 0$$
$$AC \perp BD \implies (\mathbf{a} - \mathbf{c}).(\mathbf{b} - \mathbf{d}) = 0$$

Multiply out, subtract and factorise.

$$\therefore (\mathbf{a} - \mathbf{d}).(\mathbf{c} - \mathbf{b}) = 0 \qquad \therefore AD \perp BC. \ \square$$

Solution 3.5

Let AE be the altitude of $ABCD$ through A.

Then $AE \perp BCD$.

$\therefore \quad AE \perp CD$.

But $AB \perp CD$, by hypothesis.

$\therefore \quad ABE \perp CD$.

$\therefore \quad BE \perp CD$.

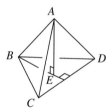

$\therefore$ BE is an altitude of BCD. Similarly CE, DE are altitudes of BCD, and so E is the orthocentre of BCD. $\square$

Solution 3.6

Let E be the orthocentre of BCD.

Then $AE \perp BCD$, since by hypothesis AE is an altitude of $ABCD$.

$\therefore \quad AE \perp CD$.

Also $BE \perp CD$, since E is the orthocentre of BCD.

$\therefore \quad ABE \perp CD$.

$\therefore \quad AB \perp CD$.

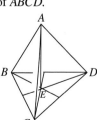

Similarly for the other 2 pairs of opposite edges. $\square$

Solution 3.7

Let L be the line through the orthocentre of, and $\perp$ to, *BCD*. If A lies on L then opposite edges are $\perp$ by Question 3.6. Conversely if opposite edges are $\perp$ then A lies on L by Question 3.5. In most cases A does not lie on L, but there are ∞ positions for A on L, and ∞^3 positions for A not on L. $\square$

4. *Perspective*

Solution 4.1

$EX \perp EY$, EZ

$\therefore EX \perp EYZ$

$\therefore EX \perp YZ$

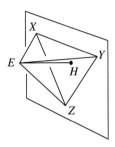

Similarly $EY \perp ZX$ and $EZ \perp XY$. Therefore pairs of opposite edges of the tetrahedron *EXYZ* are $\perp$. Therefore the altitude through E goes through the orthocentre of *XYZ* by Question 3.5. $\square$

Solution 4.2

EX, EY, EZ are perpendicular axes. The $\perp$ to *XYZ* lies in the positive quadrant relative to those axes. Therefore the orthocentre of *XYZ* lies in the interior of *XYZ*. Therefore *XYZ* is an acute-angled triangle. $\square$

Solution 4.3

$EX = EY = EZ = \frac{1}{\sqrt{2}}$. Therefore with respect to axes EX, EY, EZ the orthocentre H has coordinates

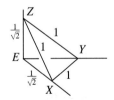

$$\frac{1}{3\sqrt{2}}(1, \ 1, \ 1). \quad \therefore EH = \sqrt{\frac{3}{18}} = \frac{1}{\sqrt{6}}. \ \square$$

Solution 4.6

As Z descends to minus infinity the spheres with diameters XZ, YZ both become the same horizontal plane through XY. The sphere with diameter XY cuts this plane in a horizontal circle through X, Y, of which the semicircle in front of the picture consists of observation points. From any of these points the picture will look like a cuboid. $\square$

5. *Desargues' Theorem*

Solution 5.1

Let Π be the plane containing the triangles $T = XYZ$, $T' = X'Y'Z'$. Suppose they are in point perspective from V.

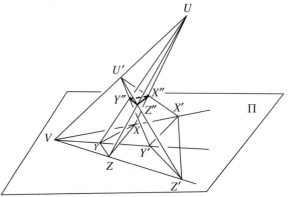

Choose a line through V not in Π, and choose 2 points U', U on this line. In the plane $VUU'XX'$ let X'' be the intersection of UX, $U'X'$. Similarly let Y'' and Z'' be the intersections of UY, $U'Y'$ and UZ, $U'Z'$, and let $T'' = X''Y''Z''$. Let L be the line of intersection of Π with the plane of T''. Let A, B, C be the intersections of L with $Y''Z''$, $Z''X''$, $X''Y''$.

Now T, T'' are in point perspective from U, and so are in line perspective by Theorem 5. Therefore YZ goes through A. Similarly $Y'Z'$ goes through A, since T', T'' are in point perspective from U'. Therefore YZ, $Y'Z'$ meet at A. Similarly the other two pairs of corresponding sides meet at B, C. Therefore T, T' are in line perspective as required.

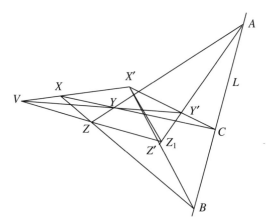

Conversely suppose T, T' are in line perspective on $L = ABC$, where YZ, $Y'Z'$ meet at A, ZX, $Z'X$ meet at B, and XY, $X'Y'$ meet at C. Let V be the intersection of XX' and YY'. Let Z_1 be the intersection of VZ with $Y'Z'$, and let $T_1 = X'Y'Z_1$. Then T, T_1 are in point perspective from V, and hence in line perspective on $L = AC$ by the above. Therefore Z_1X' goes through $L \cap ZX = B$.

$$\therefore Z_1X' = Z'X' \qquad \therefore Z_1 = Z' \qquad \therefore T_1 = T'$$

Therefore T, T' are in point perspective. $\square$

Solution 5.2

The projective coordinates $x = (x_1, x_2, x_3)$ for a point X in the plane are not all zero, and are unique up to multiplication by non-zero scalars.

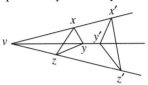

Since V, X, X' are collinear we can write

$$x' = \lambda v + \mu x, \quad \text{with } \lambda, \mu \neq 0.$$

Keeping v fixed we can rechoose the coordinates x, x' of X, X' by multiplying them by scalars λ / μ, λ.

$$\therefore \lambda x' = \lambda v + \mu \left(\frac{\lambda}{\mu} x \right)$$

$$\therefore x' = v + x$$

Similarly $y' = v + y$ and $z' = v + z$. Let

$$a = y' - z' = y - z$$
$$b = z' - x' = z - x$$
$$c = x' - y' = x - y.$$

Then A lies on YZ since a is a linear combination of y, z. Similarly A lies on $Y'Z'$, and so A is the meet of YZ, $Y'Z'$. Similarly B and C are the meets of ZX, $Z'X'$ and XY, $X'Y'$. Finally A, B, C are collinear because $a + b + c = 0$. Hence T, T' are in line perspective. $\square$

6.   *Regular polyhedra*

Solution 6.1

Polyhedron	Numbers of			Euler formula
	faces	edges	vertices	
tetrahedron	4	6	4	$4 - 6 + 4 = 2$
cube	6	12	8	$6 - 12 + 8 = 2$
octahedron	8	12	6	$8 - 12 + 6 = 2$
icosahedron	20	30	12	$20 - 30 + 12 = 2$
dodecahedron	12	30	20	$12 - 30 + 20 = 2.$

Solution 6.2

I suggest two possible ways of making the 5 regular polyhedra.

(i) A cheap way is to use drinking straws and cotton. Thread a piece of cotton through the straws representing the edges of each face, pull tight and knot. One can stop the cotton from cutting through the straws by winding sticky tape twice round each end of each straw. These make large models that are surprisingly rigid, but not very robust.

(ii) A more elegant, quick and easy way (but more expensive) is to use Polydron Frameworks, invented by Edward Harvey, and sold by Polydron International Ltd [15].   The pieces are plastic boundaries of triangles, squares, pentagons and hexagons, all of edge length 7cm, which cleverly clip together to form beautiful robust models. You can get different colours, but all my own models are green.

Solution 6.3

Join an edge AB to the centre O of the polyhedron and use Pythagoras: $c^2 = m^2 + 1$.

Suppose now that the faces are equilateral triangles.

Let AX be an altitude of a face ABC, and E the centroid (= orthocentre) of the face. Then $AX = \frac{1}{2}\sqrt{3}$.

$\therefore EX = \frac{1}{3}AX = \frac{1}{2\sqrt{3}}.$

By Pythagoras in $\triangle OEX$, $OE = \frac{1}{2}$, $OX = \frac{m}{2}$.

$\therefore m^2 = i^2 + \frac{1}{3}.$ $\square$

Solution 6.4

A regular tetrahedron of edge 1 is contained in a cube of edge $^1/_{\sqrt 2}$. Therefore the circumdiameter of the tetrahedron is the diagonal of the cube, $\sqrt 3 \, (^1/_{\sqrt 2})$. The middiameter of the tetrahedron is the distance between opposite edges, which is the same as the edge of the cube, $^1/_{\sqrt 2}$. The indiameter of the tetrahedron is given by Question 6.3:

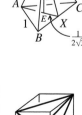

$$i = \sqrt{m^2 - \frac{1}{3}} = \sqrt{\frac{1}{2} - \frac{1}{3}} = \frac{1}{\sqrt{6}}.$$

In a regular octahedron of edge 1 the midsection is a square of edge 1. The circumdiameter of the octahedron is the distance between opposite vertices, which is the same as the diagonal of the square, $\sqrt{2}$. The middiameter of the octagon is the distance between opposite edges, which is the same as the edge of the square, 1. The indiameter is given by Question 6.3:

$$i = \sqrt{m^2 - \frac{1}{3}} = \sqrt{1 - \frac{1}{3}} = \sqrt{\frac{2}{3}}. \quad \square$$

Solution 6.5

Let *ABCDE* be a regular pentagon of edge 1.

The diagonals $AC = BE = g$. Now *CDEF* is a rhombus, since opposite edges are parallel and equal.

$$\therefore FC = FE = 1.$$

$$\therefore FA = FB = g - 1.$$

The isosceles triangles *FAB*, *ABE* are similar.

$$\therefore \frac{FA}{AB} = \frac{AB}{BE}.$$

$$\therefore \frac{g - 1}{1} = \frac{1}{g}.$$

$$\therefore g^2 - g - 1 = 0.$$

$$\therefore g = \frac{1 \pm \sqrt{5}}{2},$$

and, since $g > 0$, the positive root is chosen. $\square$

Solution 6.6

Let d, e be the diameters of the incircle, circumcircle of a regular pentagon of edge 1. Let a be the altitude: $a = \frac{1}{2}d + \frac{1}{2}e$. By Pythagoras

$$a^2 = g^2 - \frac{1}{4}$$

$$= \left(\frac{1 + \sqrt{5}}{2}\right)^2 - \frac{1}{4}$$

$$= \frac{1}{4}\left(1 + 2\sqrt{5} + 5 - 1\right)$$

$$\therefore a = \frac{1}{2}\sqrt{5 + 2\sqrt{5}}.$$

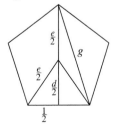

Now $e^2 = d^2 + 1$, by Pythagoras. $\therefore e = \sqrt{d^2 + 1}.$

$$\therefore d + \sqrt{d^2 + 1} = d + e = 2a = \sqrt{5 + 2\sqrt{5}}$$

$$\therefore \sqrt{d^2 + 1} = \sqrt{5 + 2\sqrt{5}} - d$$

$$\therefore d^2 + 1 = 5 + 2\sqrt{5} - 2d\sqrt{5 + 2\sqrt{5}} + d^2$$

$$\therefore 2d\sqrt{5 + 2\sqrt{5}} = 4 + 2\sqrt{5} = 2(2 + \sqrt{5})$$

$$\therefore d = \frac{2 + \sqrt{5}}{\sqrt{5 + 2\sqrt{5}}} = \frac{2 + \sqrt{5}}{\sqrt{(2 + \sqrt{5})\sqrt{5}}} = \sqrt{\frac{2 + \sqrt{5}}{\sqrt{5}}} = \sqrt{1 + \frac{2}{\sqrt{5}}}$$

$$\therefore e = \sqrt{d^2 + 1} = \sqrt{1 + \frac{2}{\sqrt{5}} + 1} = \sqrt{2 + \frac{2}{\sqrt{5}}}. \quad \square$$

Solution 6.7

Consider a cube of edge g, with rectangular axes x, y, z. Put an edge of length 1 in the middle of each face of the cube, parallel to the x, y, z-axis according as to whether the face of the cube is parallel to the (x, y), (y, z), (z, x)-planes.

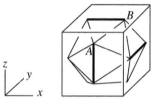

Join the closest ends of the edges in neighbouring faces. Writing the join AB in the diagram as a vector:

$$\overrightarrow{AB} = \left(\tfrac{1}{2}, \tfrac{g}{2}, \tfrac{g-1}{2}\right)$$

$$\therefore \left|\overrightarrow{AB}\right|^2 = \tfrac{1}{4}\left(1 + g^2 + (g - 1)^2\right) = \tfrac{1}{4}\left(2g^2 - 2g + 2\right) = 1, \text{ since } g^2 - g = 1.$$

Hence all the joins have length 1, and so we have an icosahedron of edge 1.

The middiameter m is the distance between opposite edges, which is the same as an edge of the cube,

$$m = g = \tfrac{1 + \sqrt{5}}{2}.$$

By Question 6.3 the circumdiameter c is given by

$$c = \sqrt{m^2 + 1} = \sqrt{\frac{1 + 2\sqrt{5} + 5}{4} + 1} = \sqrt{\frac{5 + \sqrt{5}}{2}}.$$

Again by Question 6.3 the indiameter i is given by

$$i = \sqrt{m^2 - \tfrac{1}{3}} = \sqrt{\frac{3 + \sqrt{5}}{2} - \frac{1}{3}} = \sqrt{\frac{14 + 6\sqrt{5}}{12}} = \frac{3 + \sqrt{5}}{2\sqrt{3}}. \quad \square$$

Solution 6.8

Let O be the centre of the dodecahedron and XY an edge (of length 1). By symmetry of reflection in the plane OXY the diagonal $AB \perp OXY$.

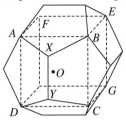

$\therefore AB \perp XY$. $\therefore AB \perp AD$, BC, since the latter are parallel to XY. Similarly $CD \perp AD$, BC. Therefore $ABCD$ is a square of edge g, since it consists of diagonals of the pentagonal faces (see Question 6.5). Similarly $ABEF$, $BCGE$ are squares. The 3 squares determine a cube of edge g.

Similarly each diagonal of a face of the dodecahedron determines a cube, and the 5 diagonals of a face determine 5 different cubes. The 5×12 edges of the cubes are determined by the 12×5 diagonals of the faces of the dodecahedron.

The circumsphere of the dodecahedron is the same as that of the cube, and therefore has diameter

$$c = \sqrt{3}g = \frac{\sqrt{3}(1 + \sqrt{5})}{2}.$$

By Question 6.3 the middiameter m of the dodecahedron is given by

$$m = \sqrt{c^2 - 1} = \sqrt{\frac{3(6 + 2\sqrt{5})}{4} - 1} = \sqrt{\frac{14 + 6\sqrt{5}}{4}} = \frac{3 + \sqrt{5}}{2}.$$

To calculate the indiameter i we join O to an altitude of a face and apply Pythagoras.

$$i = \sqrt{m^2 - d^2}, \text{ where } d = \sqrt{1 + 2/\sqrt{5}} \text{ by Question 6.6}$$

$$= \sqrt{\frac{7 + 3\sqrt{5}}{2} - \frac{5 + 2\sqrt{5}}{5}} = \sqrt{\frac{35 + 15\sqrt{5} - 10 - 4\sqrt{5}}{10}}$$

$$= \sqrt{\frac{25 + 11\sqrt{5}}{10}}. \ \square$$

Solution 6.9

The stella octangula has 24 triangular faces, 36 edges and 14 vertices. We verify that $24 - 36 + 14 = 2$. $\square$

Solution 6.10

The classification of semi-regular polyhedra having faces with ⩽ 6 edges is proved by listing all possible vertex patterns. Let t, s, p, h denote triangles, squares, pentagons and hexagons, which have internal angles 60, 90, 108 and 120 degrees. The symbol $t + 2s$, for example, indicates a vertex pattern of 1 triangle and 2 squares, which has angle sum 240, and generates the 3-prism, with global pattern $2t + 3s$. Each vertex pattern must have at least 3 faces and must have an angle sum of less than 360, which limits the choice to 19 possibilities as follows.

$2t + s$	210	×		$2t + h$	240	×
$3t + s$	270	⊙		$3t + h$	300	⊙
$4t + s$	330	⊙		$t + 2h$	300	⊙
$t + 2s$	240	⊙				
$2t + 2s$	300	⊙×		$2s + p$	288	⊙
$t + 3s$	330	⊙⊙		$s + 2p$	306	×
$2t + p$	228	×		$2s + h$	300	⊙
$3t + p$	288	⊙		$s + 2h$	330	⊙
$4t + p$	348	⊙				
$t + 2p$	276	×		$2p + h$	336	⊙
$2t + 2p$	336	⊙×				

In the above list, the first column denotes the vertex pattern, the second its angle sum, and the third indicates whether or not it generates a semi-regular polyhedron. The symbol ⊙ indicates that it does, and a × indicates that it does not. For instance $2t + s$, $2t + p$, $2t + h$ generate 4, 5, 6-pyramids, which are ruled out because the vertex at the top of a pyramid does not have the same pattern as the other vertices. Meanwhile $t + 2p$, $s + 2p$ fail because if one tries to generate a polyhedron from either of these patterns then it does not close up. The patterns $2t + 2s$, $2t + 2p$ are indicated with both ⊙ and × because, in the vertex pattern, if the triangles alternate with the other 2 faces then it does indeed generate a semi-regular polyhedron, but if they do not alternate then either it does not close up, or else generates a polyhedron with different types of vertex pattern, and hence is not semi-regular. Finally $t + 3s$ has a double symbol ⊙ ⊙ because it generates two different polyhedra, whereas all the others generate a unique polyhedron. The list of 15 marked ⊙ is shown below in detail, and agrees with the list of 15 semi-regular polyhedra described in Section 6. The list of rotation groups in the last column refers to the results of Section 7.

Vertex pattern		Global pattern	Name of semi-regular polyhedron	Euler formula $F - E + V$	Rotation group
$t + 2s$		$2t + 3s$	3-prism	$5 - 9 + 6 = 2$	S_3
$t + 3s$		$8t + 18s$	mitred cube	$26 - 48 + 24 = 2$	S_4
$t + 3s$		$8t + 18s$	twisted mitred cube	$26 - 48 + 24 = 2$	D_4
$2t + 2s$		$8t + 6s$	midedge cube	$14 - 24 + 12 = 2$	S_4
$3t + s$		$8t + 2s$	4-antiprism	$10 - 16 + 8 = 2$	D_4
$4t + s$		$32t + 6s$	snub cube	$38 - 60 + 24 = 2$	S_4
$2t + 2p$		$20t + 12p$	midedge dodecahedron	$32 - 60 + 30 = 2$	A_5
$3t + p$		$10t + 2p$	5-antiprism	$12 - 20 + 10 = 2$	D_5
$4t + p$		$80t + 12p$	snub dodecahedron	$92 - 150 + 60 = 2$	A_5
$t + 2h$		$4t + 4h$	truncated tetrahedron	$8 - 18 + 12 = 2$	A_4
$3t + h$		$12t + 2h$	6-antiprism	$14 - 24 + 12 = 2$	D_6
$2s + p$		$5s + 2p$	5-prism	$7 - 15 + 10 = 2$	D_5
$s + 2h$		$6s + 8h$	truncated octahedron	$14 - 36 + 24 = 2$	S_4
$2s + h$		$6s + 2h$	6-prism	$8 - 18 + 12 = 2$	D_6
$p + 2h$		$12p + 20h$	buckminsterfullerene	$32 - 90 + 60 = 2$	A_5.

This completes the classification of semi-regular polyhedra having faces with at most 6 edges.

Solution 6.13

The rhombic dodecahedron has 12 faces, 24 edges and 14 vertices. We verify that

$$12 - 24 + 14 = 2. \quad \square$$

7. Rotation Groups

Solution 7.1

Given an n-prism P, $n \neq 4$, the plane halfway between top and bottom meets the sides in an n-gon Q. Any rotation of P induces a rotation of Q, and vice versa. Therefore the rotation group of P is the same as that of Q, namely D_n.

The case $n = 4$ is exceptional because the 4-prism is a cube, and so there are extra symmetries, which are not in D_4, that rotate the top and bottom of the cube onto the sides. Therefore the rotation group is S_4 rather than its subgroup D_4.

Given an *n*-antiprism *A*, $n \neq 3$, the halfway plane meets the sides in a 2*n*-gon *B*. Let *C* be an *n*-gon joining every other vertex of *B*. Then any rotation of *A* induces a rotation of *C*, and vice versa. Therefore the rotation group of *A* is the same as that

of *C*, namely D_n. The case $n = 3$ is exceptional because the 3-antiprism is an octahedron, and so there are extra symmetries, which are not in D_3, that rotate the top and bottom onto the sides. Therefore the rotation group is again S_4 rather than its subgroup D_3. □

Solution 7.2

In the twisted mitred cube *T* there is a unique octagonal ring of 8 squares (as opposed to the mitred cube in which there are 3 such rings). Therefore any rotation must send this ring to itself. Regarding this ring as horizontal, let *S* be a horizontal square joining the

midpoints of every other vertical edge of the ring. Then every rotation of *T* induces a rotation of *S*, and vice versa. Hence the rotation group of *T* is the same as that of *S*, namely D_4. □

Solution 7.3

The multiplication table for A_4 is:

	1	12.34	13.24	14.23	123	132	124	142	134	143	234	243
1	1	12.34	13.24	14.23	123	132	124	142	134	143	234	243
12.34	12.34	1	14.23	13.24	134	234	143	243	123	124	132	142
13.24	13.24	14.23	1	12.34	243	124	132	134	142	234	143	123
14.23	14.23	13.24	12.34	1	142	143	234	123	243	132	124	134
123	123	243	142	134	132	1	14.23	234	124	12.34	13.24	143
132	132	143	234	124	1	123	134	13.24	14.23	243	142	12.34
124	124	234	143	132	13.24	243	142	1	12.34	123	134	14.23
142	142	134	123	243	143	14.23	1	124	234	13.24	12.34	132
134	134	142	243	123	234	12.34	13.24	132	143	1	14.23	124
143	143	132	124	234	14.23	142	243	12.34	1	134	123	13.24
234	234	124	132	143	12.34	134	123	14.23	13.24	142	243	1
243	243	123	134	142	124	13.24	12.34	143	132	14.23	1	234

Writing the (2,2)-cycles first reveals that they, together with the identity, form an abelian subgroup of order 4 (isomorphic to D_2). □

Solution 7.4

Each vertex of the mitred tetrahedron lies on 2 triangles, one coming from a vertex of the tetrahedron and the other from a face, separated by 2 squares coming from edges of the tetrahedron. Therefore the mitred tetrahedron has vertex pattern $2t + 2s$, global pattern $8t + 6s$, with 14 faces, 24 edges and 12 vertices, the same as the midedge cube (see Question 6.10). The identification can be visualised from the standard embedding of a tetrahedron in a cube. The rotation of order 2 about the join of opposite vertices is induced by the rotation of the cube about the join of midpoints of opposite edges, but is not induced by any rotation of the tetrahedron because it interchanges 2 triangles, one derived from a vertex and the other from a face. Therefore the rotation group is S_4 induced from the cube, rather than the subgroup A_4 from the tetrahedron. $\square$

Solution 7.5

The rhombus has 3 rotations ω, a, β of order 2 about the axes shown. The multiplication table is the same as that of D_2, which is abelian because the table is symmetric about the leading diagonal.

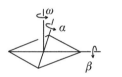

$$D_2 = \begin{array}{c|cccc} & 1 & \omega & \alpha & \beta \\ \hline 1 & 1 & \omega & \alpha & \beta \\ \omega & \omega & 1 & \beta & \alpha \\ \alpha & \alpha & \beta & 1 & \omega \\ \beta & \beta & \alpha & \omega & 1 \end{array} \qquad \square$$

8.   *Tessellations and sphere packings*

Solution 8.1

Use the cubic tessellation, and fill each cube, as in Question 2.7, with 3 Dehn's tetrahedra and 3 mirror images. $\square$

Solution 8.2

Use Question 2.9. $\square$

Solution 8.3

Use Question 2.10. $\square$

Solution 8.4

In the cubic lattice place a tetrahedron inside each cube so that its vertices are at odd points of the lattice (points whose integer coordinates have an odd sum). Then at each even point there will be 8 right-angled tetrahedra, whose union is a regular octahedron of edge $\sqrt{2}$. Thus 1 octahedron corresponds to 8 right-angled tetrahedra, and hence to 2 of the regular tetrahedra. $\square$

Solution 8.5

A barrow boy's tetrahedron, of edge 4, contains $1 + 3 + 6 + 10 = 20$ spheres.

$\square$

Solution 8.6

Suppose the spheres have radius 1. The distance between two rows in a layer of A is 2, while that in B is $\sqrt{3}$. Therefore in a large region the ratio of numbers of spheres in a layer of A to that in B is $\sqrt{3}/2$.

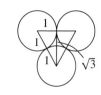

In the second layer of A each sphere sits on 4 spheres, and their centres form a square pyramid of edge 2. An altitude of a sloping face of the pyramid is $\sqrt{3}$, and hence the height of the pyramid is $\sqrt{2}$. Therefore the height between two layers is $\sqrt{2}$. Meanwhile in B we use a triangular pyramid because each sphere sits on 3 spheres. The height of a triangular pyramid is $2\sqrt{2/3}$,

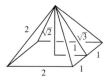

and so that is the height between two layers of B. Hence the ratio between heights of layers in A and B is $\sqrt{2}/(2\sqrt{2/3}) = \sqrt{3}/2$. Therefore the ratio between the number of layers in A and B is $2/\sqrt{3}$. Therefore the number of spheres in A and B is the same, confirming Theorem 8.2. $\square$

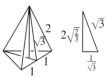

Solution 8.8

The rhombic-trapezoid dodecahedron has 12 faces, 24 edges and 14 vertices, the same as the rhombic dodecahedron. 2 vertices each have 3 rhombi meeting at their larger angles; 6 vertices each have 1 rhombus and 2 trapezia meeting at their larger angles; and 6 vertices each have 2 rhombi and 2 trapezia meeting at their smaller angles. The rotation group is D_3, induced by rotations of the triangle joining the midpoints of the 3 longest edges. $\square$

Solution 8.9

The tessellation induced by the hexagonal packing is a modification of the barrow boy's tessellation. In the latter each rhombic dodecahedron is stacked so that the line joining two vertices where 3 rhombi meet is vertical. There are 3 rhombi at the top, 3 at the bottom, and 6 round the sides. The horizontal midplane cuts the 6 side faces in a hexagon.

The main differing feature of the hexagonal packing is that there is a reflectional symmetry in the midplane. Hence a cell of the induced tessellation is the same below the midplane as the rhombic dodecahedron, and above the midplane is its reflection. Therefore each side rhombus is replaced by a trapezium.

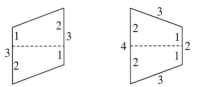

Thus the cell has 3 rhombi at the top, 3 at the bottom, and 6 trapezia round the sides, forming the rhombic-trapezoid dodecahedron. □

9. Conics

Solution 9.1

□

Solution 9.2

Let H be the conic, the intersection between the plane and cone. The condition $\alpha > \beta$ implies that the plane meets both parts of the cone as shown.

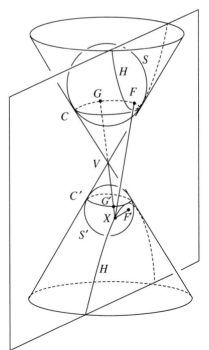

Let S, S' be the two spheres touching both the cone in circles C, C' and the plane in points F, F'. Let V be the vertex of the cone. Given $X \in H$, let VX cut C, C' in G, G'. Then

$$XF = XG, \text{ being tangents from } X \text{ to } S$$

$$\text{and } XF' = XG', \text{ being tangents from } X \text{ to } S'.$$

$\therefore XF - XF' = XG - XG' = GG' = $ constant, the distance between C, C'. Therefore H is a hyperbola with foci F, F'. $\square$

Solution 9.3
Let H be the hyperbola, with foci F, F' at $(\pm c, 0)$.

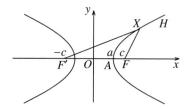

Let $A = (a, 0)$ be the positive vertex. Let X be a point on H. When $X = A$ then $AF' - AF = (a + c) - (c - a) = 2a$.
When $X = (x, y)$ then $\left| \sqrt{(x + c)^2 + y^2} - \sqrt{(x - c)^2 + y^2} \right| = 2a$, by constancy.
Square:

$$\left(x^2 + y^2 + c^2 + 2cx\right) + \left(x^2 + y^2 + c^2 - 2cx\right)$$

$$- 2\sqrt{(x^2 + y^2 + c^2 + 2cx)(x^2 + y^2 + c^2 - 2cx)} = 4a^2$$

$$\therefore \sqrt{(x^2 + y^2 + c^2)^2 - 4c^2x^2} = \left(x^2 + y^2 + c^2\right) - 2a^2$$

Square:

$$\left(x^2 + y^2 + c^2\right)^2 - 4c^2x^2 = \left(x^2 + y^2 + c^2\right)^2 - 4a^2\left(x^2 + y^2 + c^2\right) + 4a^4$$

$$\therefore c^2x^2 - a^2\left(x^2 + y^2 + c^2\right) = -a^4$$

$$\therefore \left(c^2 - a^2\right)x^2 - a^2y^2 = a^2\left(c^2 - a^2\right)$$

Let $b^2 = c^2 - a^2$, where $c > a$, and so $b > 0$. Then $b^2x^2 - a^2y^2 = a^2b^2$.

$$\therefore \left(\frac{x}{a}\right)^2 - \left(\frac{y}{b}\right)^2 = 1. \square$$

Solution 9.4

Let Π be the plane, and P the conic of intersection of Π with the cone. The condition $\alpha = \beta$ implies that Π is parallel to a generator of the cone, and therefore meets only one part of the cone.

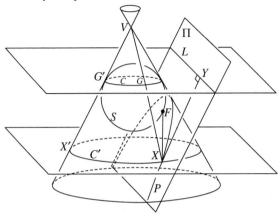

Let S be the sphere touching the cone in a circle C and Π in a point F. Let the horizontal plane containing C meet Π in the line L. Given $X \in P$, let the horizontal plane through X meet the cone in a circle C'. Let V be the vertex of the cone, and let VX meet C in G. Let the generator of the cone parallel to Π meet C, C' in G', X'. Let XY be the $\perp$ from X onto L. Then

$XY = X'G'$, being parallel segments between horizontal planes

$\quad = XG$, being the distance between the horizontal circles C, C'

$\quad = XF$, being tangents from X to S.

Therefore X is equidistant from F and L. Therefore the locus of X is a parabola. $\square$

Solution 9.5

Suppose the parabola P has focus $F = (a, 0)$ and directrix $x = -a$.

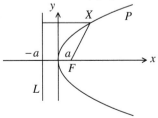

Let $X = (x, y)$ be a point on P. Then

$$x + a = \sqrt{(x - a)^2 + y^2}.$$

Square:

$$x^2 + 2ax + a^2 = x^2 - 2ax + a^2 + y^2$$

$$\therefore y^2 = 4ax. \quad \square$$

Solution 9.6

Let E be the eye, and C the circle. Let O be the centre, and a the radius, of C, and Π the plane containing C. Let EX be the $\perp$ from E onto Π. Let XO meet C in the diameter YZ, and let AB be the $\perp$ diameter. Let EM be the angle bisector of $\angle YEZ$.

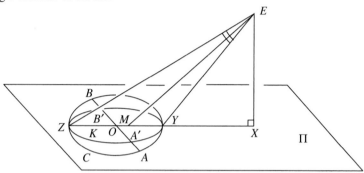

Let Q be the circular cone with vertex E and axis EM through Y and Z. Then Q meets Π in an ellipse K, by Theorem 9.1, with major axis YZ and touching C at Y, Z. Let Q meet AB in A', B'. Then $A'B'$ is the minor axis of K. Let $b = OA' = OB'$. The whole picture is symmetrical about the plane EXY. Let f be the linear expansion of $\mathbb{R}^3$ that keeps the plane EXY pointwise fixed, and expands the axis AB by a factor a/b.

We claim $f(K) = C$. For, with respect to axes OY, OA, the ellipse K has equation

$$\left(\frac{x}{a}\right)^2 + \left(\frac{y}{b}\right)^2 = 1, \text{ by Theorem 9.2.}$$

Now f maps (x, y) to (x, y') where $y' = \frac{a}{b} y$. $\quad \therefore \frac{y}{b} = \frac{y'}{a}$. Therefore $f(K) = C$ because

$$\left(\frac{x}{a}\right)^2 + \left(\frac{y'}{a}\right)^2 = 1, \text{ and so } x^2 + y'^2 = a^2.$$

Similarly f maps circles to ellipses, and hence f maps the circular cone Q onto an elliptical cone $f(Q)$. More precisely EM is the axis of the cone Q, and if Σ is a plane $\perp EM$, then Q meets Σ in a circle C', and Q is the cone on C'. Therefore $f(Q)$ is the cone on the ellipse $f(C')$, and is therefore an elliptical cone. But $Q \supset K$ and so $f(Q) \supset f(K) = C$. Therefore C looks elliptical to the eye E. $\quad \square$

Solution 9.7

The outside of a crescent moon is a semicircle from A to B, which is half the circular boundary C of the moon seen from the Earth. The inside of the crescent moon is the visible half of that circle bounding the half of the moon lit by the sun. By Question 9.6 that circle looks to the eye as an ellipse E touching C at A and B. Therefore the crescent moon is half the region between the circle C and the inscribed ellipse E. When the complementary region inside C is lit it is called a *gibbous* moon.

Today most artists are not aware of these facts, and so if they have to paint a crescent moon they tend to paint the inside as an arc of another (larger) circle, thereby creating nonzero angles at A and B, which look coarse to the eye compared with the delicacy of the points of the real crescent moon. □

10. *Inversion*

Solution 10.1

The left diagram shows by isosceles triangles that the angle subtended by a chord in a circle is half that subtended at the centre O. The right diagram shows that the latter equals the angle between the chord and tangent.

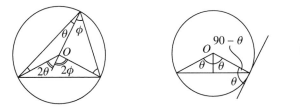

□

Solution 10.2

Let f be inversion with respect to the sphere centre O and radius $k > 0$. Suppose f maps sphere A to sphere A'.

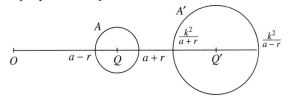

Let Q be the centre of A, r be the radius of A, and Q' be the centre of A'. Let $a = OQ$ and $a' = OQ'$. Then OQ meets A in points at distances $a + r$, $a - r$ from O. Therefore OQ meets A' in points at distances $k^2/(a + r)$, $k^2/(a - r)$ from O.

$$\therefore a' = \frac{1}{2}\left(\frac{k^2}{a + r} + \frac{k^2}{a - r}\right)$$

$$= \frac{k^2 a}{a^2 - r^2}$$

$$\neq \frac{k^2}{a}, \text{ the distance from } O \text{ to the image } f(Q) \text{ of } Q,$$

because $a^2 \neq a^2 - r^2$, since $r > 0$. Therefore $f(Q) \neq Q'$. □

11. *Cross-ratios*

Solution 11.1

In a complete quadrilateral the 4 lines a, b, c, d meet in 6 vertices A, B, C, D, E, F, and the 3 diagonals $p = EF$, $q = CD$, $r = AB$ meet in the 3 diagonal vertices P, Q, R.

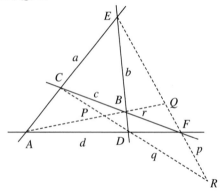

Let $x = (APBQ)$

$= (CPDR)$, by projection from E

$= (BPAQ)$, by projection from F

$= \dfrac{BP.AQ}{BQ.AP}$

$= \left(\dfrac{AP.BQ}{AQ.BP}\right)^{-1}$

$= \dfrac{1}{x}.$

$$\therefore x^2 = 1.$$

But $x \neq 1$ because the 4 points are distinct.

$$\therefore x = -1. \quad \square$$

12. *Rings of spheres*

Solution 12.1

It suffices to produce a counterexample. Consider Dehn's tetrahedron $ABCD$, inscribed in the unit cube. If there were a midsphere then it would meet each face in its incircle. Therefore the incircles of the 4 faces would meet pairwise at the points where the midsphere touches the edges. The incircle of ABC meets BC at X.

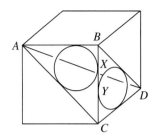

Let the radius of the incircle be $x = BX$. Then the lengths of the tangents are as shown. Hence $2(1 - x) = AC = \sqrt{2}$ and so $x = 1 - \frac{1}{\sqrt{2}}$. Similarly, the incircle of BCD meets BC at Y, where $CY = x$. $\therefore X \neq Y$, giving a contradiction. Therefore $ABCD$ has no midsphere. $\square$

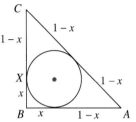

Solution 12.2

(i) $\Rightarrow$ (ii) Suppose the sums of opposite edges are equal. For each face, define the *inline* of that face to be the line $\perp$ to the face through the incentre (the intersections of the angle bisectors). Given a face XYZ, let I be the incentre and let IA, IB, IC be the perpendiculars onto the edges YZ, ZX, XY and let

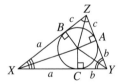

$$a = XB = XC$$
$$b = YC = YA$$
$$c = ZA = ZB.$$

The incircle of XYZ goes through A, B, C, with centre I and radius $IA = IB = IC$. Moreover

$$a - b = (a + c) - (b + c) = y - x.$$

We claim that the incircle of XYT also goes through C because, if $\xi = XT$, $\eta = YT$, $\zeta = ZT$ then $x + \xi = y + \eta$ by hypothesis (i).

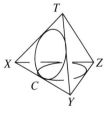

$$\therefore \xi - \eta = y - x = a - b.$$

Therefore C is where the incircle of XYT touches XY. Let Π be the plane $\perp XY$ through C. Then $\Pi \supset CI$ because $CI \perp XY$. $\therefore I \in \Pi$. Also Π contains the inline of XYZ because the latter is $\perp XYZ$, and therefore $\perp XY$. Similarly Π contains the inline of XYT. Hence the inlines of XYZ, XYT meet. Similarly the 4 inlines meet pairwise. But no 2 are coplanar. Therefore all 4 are concurrent, at M say. Since M lies on the inline of XYZ it is equidistant from the edges XY, YZ, ZX. Similarly M is equidistant from all 6 edges. Therefore the sphere centre M and radius MA is the midsphere of $XYZT$ touching all 6 edges.

(ii) $\Rightarrow$ (iii) Assume there exists a midsphere.

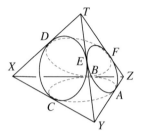

Let the midsphere touch XT, YT, ZT in D, E, F. Then $XB = XC = XD$ since they are all tangents from X to the midsphere. Therefore the sphere centre X, radius XC, cuts the edges XZ, XY, XT orthogonally at B, C, D. Similarly the sphere centre Y, radius YC, cuts the edges YX, YZ, YT orthogonally at C, A, E. Therefore the 2 spheres touch at C. Similarly there exist spheres centred at Z, T such that the 4 spheres all touch each other at the 6 points where the midsphere touches the 6 edges.

(iii) $\Rightarrow$ (i) Assume there are 4 spheres centred at X, Y, Z, T all touching one another. Let r_X, r_Y, r_Z, r_T be their radii. Then

$$XY = r_X + r_Y \text{ and } ZT = r_Z + r_T$$

$$\therefore XY + ZT = r_X + r_Y + r_Z + r_T$$

$$= XZ + YT = XT + YZ, \text{ similarly.}$$

Therefore the 3 sums of opposite edges are equal. $\square$

Solution 12.3

If a 4-ring of spheres is interlockable then the contact circle is orthogonal to the spheres by Theorem 12.6, and so the centres of the spheres lie on the tangents to the contact circle at the contact points, and hence lie in the plane of the contact circle.

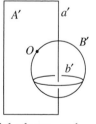

Given interlocking 4-rings, α, β let a, b denote their contact circles and A, B the planes containing them. We have to show $A \perp B$. Invert in a contact point O on a. Then the two spheres touching at O become two parallel planes, and a becomes a line a' perpendicular to those planes. Since A contains O, it inverts into itself, $A = A'$. Therefore A' is the plane containing O and a'. Meanwhile β inverts into a 4-ring β' consisting of 4 equal spheres touching the 2 planes, with contact circle b' lying midway between the planes. B inverts into the sphere B' containing b' and O, and a' is a diameter of B' because it is $\perp b'$ and goes through the centre of b'. Therefore A' is orthogonal to B'. Therefore $A \perp B$, since inversion is conformal by Theorem 10.4. $\square$

13. *Areas of spheres and volumes of balls*

Solution 13.1

Let C be a cone of height h on a base B of any shape. Let C_x be the section at height x below the vertex. Then C_x equals B scaled down by a factor $\frac{x}{h}$.

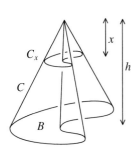

$$\therefore C = \int_0^h B\left(\frac{x}{h}\right)^2 dx$$

$$= \frac{B}{h^2} \int_0^h x^2 dx$$

$$= \frac{B}{h^2}\left(\frac{h^3}{3}\right) = \tfrac{1}{3} \times \text{base} \times \text{height}. \ \square$$

Solution 13.2

Volume of slice =

$$\pi (r \cos \theta)^2 d (r \sin \theta) = \pi (r \cos \theta)^2 r \cos \theta \, d\theta = \pi r^3 \cos^3 \theta d\theta.$$

$$\therefore \text{ volume of sphere} = \int_{-\pi/2}^{\pi/2} \pi r^3 \cos^3 \theta \, d\theta$$

$$= 2\pi r^3 \int_0^{\pi/2} \cos\theta\left(1 - \sin^2 \theta\right)d\theta$$

$$= 2\pi r^3 \left[\sin \theta - \tfrac{1}{3} \sin^3 \theta\right]_0^{\pi/2}$$

$$= 2\pi r^3 \left[1 - \tfrac{1}{3}\right]$$

$$= \tfrac{4}{3}\pi r^3. \ \square$$

14. *Map projections*

Solution 14.1

Central projection maps $(\phi, -\theta) \rightarrow (r \cot \theta, \phi)$, in polar coordinates.

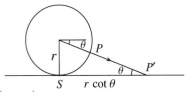

Therefore the small rectangle at $(\phi, -\theta)$ induced by the small increments $(d\phi, d\theta)$ has sides

$$(r \cos \theta \, d\phi, -r \, d\theta),$$

and is mapped to the small rectangle

$$(r \cot \theta \, d\phi, d (r \cot \theta)) = (r \cot \theta \, d\phi, -r \operatorname{cosec}^2 \theta \, d\theta).$$

Therefore the horizontal sides are expanded by $\operatorname{cosec} \theta$, and the vertical sides by $\operatorname{cosec}^2 \theta$, giving a ratio of $\operatorname{cosec} \theta$. $\square$

Solution 14.2
Stereographic projection maps $(\phi, \theta) \to (2r\tan(\frac{\pi}{4} + \frac{\theta}{2}), \phi)$, in polar coordinates.

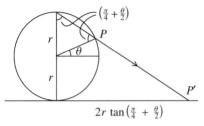

Therefore the small rectangle at (ϕ, θ) induced by the small increments $(d\phi, d\theta)$ has sides

$$(r\cos\theta \, d\phi, \, r \, d\theta)$$

and is mapped to the small rectangle

$$\left(2r\tan\left(\tfrac{\pi}{4} + \tfrac{\theta}{2}\right)d\phi, \, d\left(2r\tan\left(\tfrac{\pi}{4} + \tfrac{\theta}{2}\right)\right)\right) = \left(2r\tan\left(\tfrac{\pi}{4} + \tfrac{\theta}{2}\right)d\phi, \, r\sec^2\left(\tfrac{\pi}{4} + \tfrac{\theta}{2}\right)d\theta\right).$$

Now

$$\sin\left(\tfrac{\pi}{4} + \tfrac{\theta}{2}\right) = \sin\tfrac{\pi}{4}\cos\tfrac{\theta}{2} + \cos\tfrac{\pi}{4}\sin\tfrac{\theta}{2} = \tfrac{1}{\sqrt{2}}\left(\cos\tfrac{\theta}{2} + \sin\tfrac{\theta}{2}\right)$$

$$\cos\left(\tfrac{\pi}{4} + \tfrac{\theta}{2}\right) = \cos\tfrac{\pi}{4}\cos\tfrac{\theta}{2} - \sin\tfrac{\pi}{4}\sin\tfrac{\theta}{2} = \tfrac{1}{\sqrt{2}}\left(\cos\tfrac{\theta}{2} - \sin\tfrac{\theta}{2}\right).$$

Therefore the horizontal multiplier is

$$\frac{2\tan\left(\tfrac{\pi}{4} + \tfrac{\theta}{2}\right)}{\cos\theta} = \frac{2\frac{\cos\frac{\theta}{2} + \sin\frac{\theta}{2}}{\cos\frac{\theta}{2} - \sin\frac{\theta}{2}}}{\cos^2\tfrac{\theta}{2} - \sin^2\tfrac{\theta}{2}}$$

$$= \frac{2}{\left(\cos\tfrac{\theta}{2} - \sin\tfrac{\theta}{2}\right)^2}$$

$$= \sec^2\left(\frac{\pi}{4} + \frac{\theta}{2}\right),$$

which the same as the vertical multiplier. $\square$

15. *Knotting*

Solution 15.1
We have to show that a knot K has code 3 if and only if it can be 3-coloured. Suppose K can be 3-coloured with colours 0,1,2. If only one colour is used at a crossing then trivially the overpass is the average of the underpasses. If 3 colours are used at a crossing then one of 3 cases holds: $0 + 1 = 4 \pmod 3$, $1 + 2 = 0 \pmod 3$ or $2 + 0 = 2 \pmod 3$. In each case the overpass is the average of the 2 underpasses modulo 3. Therefore K has code 3. Conversely if K has code 3 then the labelling is a 3-colouring. $\square$

Solution 15.2

We show the product of the trefoil and the square knot has code 3 by labelling the trefoil appropriately with the integers mod 3 and labelling the square knot all the same. Similarly show it has code 5 by labelling the square knot appropriately with the integers mod 5 and labelling the trefoil all the same. □

Solution 15.3

The first two cases of the trefoil and the square knot have already been done. In each of the other dozen cases we start by labelling one crossing with 0,1,2, then the next crossing with 1,2,3, and so on preserving the averages until the penultimate crossing (indicated by an arrow) which gives an equation for the code p, which of course is prime. The last crossing is satisfied automatically (as can be deduced from the solution to 15.4), and thus provides a convenient check on the computation.

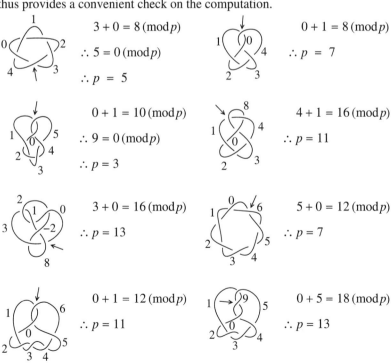

$3 + 0 = 8 \,(\mathrm{mod}\,p)$

$\therefore 5 = 0 \,(\mathrm{mod}\,p)$

$\therefore p = 5$

$0 + 1 = 8 \,(\mathrm{mod}\,p)$

$\therefore p = 7$

$0 + 1 = 10 \,(\mathrm{mod}\,p)$

$\therefore 9 = 0 \,(\mathrm{mod}\,p)$

$\therefore p = 3$

$4 + 1 = 16 \,(\mathrm{mod}\,p)$

$\therefore p = 11$

$3 + 0 = 16 \,(\mathrm{mod}\,p)$

$\therefore p = 13$

$5 + 0 = 12 \,(\mathrm{mod}\,p)$

$\therefore p = 7$

$0 + 1 = 12 \,(\mathrm{mod}\,p)$

$\therefore p = 11$

$0 + 5 = 18 \,(\mathrm{mod}\,p)$

$\therefore p = 13$

$8 + 1 = -6 \,(\mathrm{mod}\,p)$

$\therefore 15 = 0 \,(\mathrm{mod}\,p)$

$\therefore p = 3 \text{ or } 5$

$1 + 4 = -12 \,(\mathrm{mod}\,p)$

$\therefore p = 17$

$7 + 12 = 0 \,(\mathrm{mod}\,p)$

$\therefore p = 19$

$8 + 13 = 0 \,(\mathrm{mod}\,p)$

$\therefore 21 = 0 \,(\mathrm{mod}\,p)$

$\therefore p = 3 \text{ or } 7. \quad \square$

Solution 15.4

Given any knot K, let $a_1, a_2, \ldots, a_n$ be the arcs going round the knot, and let $c_1, c_2, \ldots, c_n$ be the crossings such that, for each i, c_i is the front end of a_i. Define an $n \times n$ matrix M with rows corresponding to the crossings c_i and columns corresponding to the arcs a_j, such that

$$M_{ij} = \begin{cases} 1, & \text{if } c_i \text{ has underpass } a_j \\ -2, & \text{if } c_i \text{ has overpass } a_j \\ 0, & \text{otherwise.} \end{cases}$$

Define D by omitting the last row and column of M. Let $d = |D|$, the determinant of D. We claim that the codes of K are the prime factors of d.

Example: the square knot

$$M = \begin{vmatrix} 1 & 1 & 0 & -2 \\ -2 & 1 & 1 & 0 \\ 0 & -2 & 1 & 1 \\ 1 & 0 & -2 & 1 \end{vmatrix} \qquad \therefore D = \begin{vmatrix} 1 & 1 & 0 \\ -2 & 1 & 1 \\ 0 & -2 & 1 \end{vmatrix}$$

Expanding by the first row,

$$d = \begin{vmatrix} 1 & 1 \\ -2 & 1 \end{vmatrix} - \begin{vmatrix} -2 & 1 \\ 0 & 1 \end{vmatrix} = 3 - (-2) = 5.$$

And 5 is indeed the code of the square knot, as we showed in Section 15.

Proof of the claim

First notice that d is odd because mod 2

$$D = \begin{vmatrix} 1 & 1 & 0 & 0 & \dots & 0 & 0 \\ 0 & 1 & 1 & 0 & \dots & 0 & 0 \\ \vdots & & & & & & \vdots \\ 0 & 0 & 0 & 0 & \dots & 1 & 1 \\ 0 & 0 & 0 & 0 & \dots & 0 & 1 \end{vmatrix}$$

Therefore $d = 1 \pmod 2$. Suppose p is a code of K. Choose a labelling of K with integers mod p. Let x_i be the label on a_i, and let

$$x = \begin{pmatrix} x_1 \\ x_2 \\ \vdots \\ x_n \end{pmatrix}.$$

Then condition (2) of the labelling implies $Mx = 0 \pmod p$, because each row of M corresponds to a crossing, and multiplied into x adds the labels on the 2 underpasses of that crossing, minus twice the label on the overpass. By subtracting x_n from each label we can relabel so that $x_n = 0$, while still preserving condition (2). Let y be the $(n-1)$-column obtained by leaving off the last term of x:

$$y = \begin{pmatrix} x_1 \\ \vdots \\ x_{n-1} \end{pmatrix}, \text{ and } x = \begin{pmatrix} y \\ \hline 0 \end{pmatrix}.$$

Let c be the $(n-1)$-column consisting of the last column of M without its bottom term. Let r be the last row of M.

$$\therefore M = \left(\begin{array}{c|c} D & c \\ \hline r \end{array} \right) \qquad \therefore Mx = \left(\begin{array}{c|c} D & c \\ \hline r \end{array} \right) \begin{pmatrix} y \\ \hline 0 \end{pmatrix} = \begin{pmatrix} Dy \\ \hline rx \end{pmatrix}.$$

$$\therefore Dy = 0 \pmod p, \text{ since } Mx = 0 \pmod p.$$

But $y \neq 0 \pmod p$, by condition (1) of the labelling, so D is singular $\pmod p$.

$$\therefore d = |D| = 0 \pmod p.$$

$\therefore d$ is a multiple of p. In other words p is a prime factor of d. Therefore the codes of K are prime factors of d.

Conversely let p be a prime factor of d. Then $d = 0 \pmod p$. Therefore the columns of D are linearly dependent $\pmod p$. In other words there exists a non-zero $(n-1)$-column y of integers mod p such that $Dy = 0 \pmod p$.

Let $x = \begin{pmatrix} y \\ \hline 0 \end{pmatrix}$. Then $(D \,|\, c)x = (D \,|\, c)\begin{pmatrix} y \\ \hline 0 \end{pmatrix} = Dy = 0 \pmod p$.

Now $|M| = 0$ because the columns of M add to zero, since each row contains 1,1,-2 and the rest of the terms zero. Therefore the rows of M are linearly dependent. But the first $n-1$ rows are independent because $|D| \neq 0$, since d is odd. Therefore the last row r of M is dependent on the rows of $\left(D \mid c \right)$. Therefore $rx = 0 \pmod p$, since $\left(D \mid c \right)x = 0 \pmod p$.

$$\therefore Mx = \left(\frac{D \mid c}{r} \right) x = 0 \pmod p.$$

Therefore x gives a labelling of K satisfying conditions (1) and (2). Hence p is a code of K. We have shown that the codes of K are precisely the prime factors of d, and so K has only a finite number of codes. $\square$

Solution 15.5

| expand | roll round 180° like a smoke ring | rotate 90° | contract | $\square$ |

16. *Linking*

Solution 16.1

$L = 2.$

Yes, equal.

Proof:

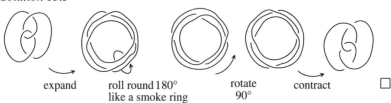

Solution 16.2

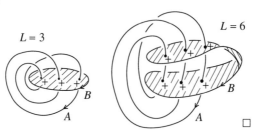

$L = 3$

$L = 6$

$\square$

Solution 16.3

The left hand diagram shows that the Whitehead link has $L = 0$.

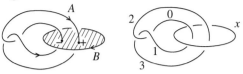

Suppose that it had code p. Then $0 + 1 = 2x = 2 + 3 \pmod{p}$. Therefore $4 = 0 \pmod{p}$, contradicting that p is odd. Therefore it has no codes. Unlinked curves, on the other hand, have all codes. Therefore the Whitehead link is linked. $\square$

Solution 16.4

Borromean rings

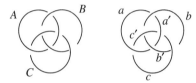

The diagram shows 3 curves of which any pair are unlinked. To show that together they are linked we prove that they have no codes. Suppose that the Borromean rings had code p, and was labelled as shown. Then $a + a' = 2b \pmod{p}$ by condition (2), and similarly $a + a' = 2b' \pmod{p}$. Therefore $2b = 2b' \pmod{p}$, and hence $b = b' \pmod{p}$ since p is odd. Similarly $a = a' \pmod{p}$. Therefore $2a = 2b \pmod{p}$, and so $a = b \pmod{p}$. Similarly $b = c \pmod{p}$, violating condition (1), and giving a contradiction. Therefore the Borromean rings have no codes. On the other hand unlinked curves can be moved apart and so have all codes. Therefore the Borromean rings are linked, although pairwise unlinked. $\square$

BIBLIOGRAPHY

1. L B Alberti, *Della pittura*, Firenze, 1435.

2. E Artin, Zur Isotopie zweidimensionaler Flächen im $\mathbb{R}^4$, *Abh. aus dem Math. Sem. Hamburg* IV (1926) pp. 174-177.

3. F H Bool, B Ernst, J R Kist, J L Locher and F Wierda, *Escher: the complete graphic work*, Thames and Hudson, 1992.

4. R Courant and H Robbins, *What is mathematics?*, OUP, 1941.

5. H S M Coxeter, Interlocked rings of spheres, *Scripta Mathematica*, 18 (1952), pp. 113-121.

6. H S M Coxeter, *Introduction to geometry*, Wiley, 1961.

7. *Encyclopedia of World Art*, McGraw-Hill, 1966, Plate 87.

8. *Euclid: Elements*, (trans. T L Heath), 1908, Reprinted Dover, New York, 1956.

9. M Fox, Chains, froths and a ten-bead necklace, *Math. Gazette*, **84** (July 2000) pp. 242-259.

10. T C Hales, A computer verification of the Kepler conjecture, *Proc. Int. Congress of Math.*, Vol III, Beijing (2002) pp. 795-804.

11. D Hilbert and S Cohn-Vossen, *Geometry and the imagination*, AMS, Chelsea, 1952.

12. G A Jennings, *Modern geometry with applications*, Springer, 1994.

13. F Klein, *Lectures on the icosahedron*, Kegan Paul, London, 1913.

14. W B R Lickorish, *An introduction to knot theory*, Springer, 1997.

15. Polydron International Ltd., Kemble, Cirencester, Glos. GL7 6BA.

16. F Soddy, The hexlet, *Nature*, **138** (1936) p. 958 and **139** (1937) p. 154.

17. *Teaching and learning geometry 11-19*, Report of a Royal Society and Joint Mathematical Council working group, 2001.

18. E C Zeeman, Unknotting spheres in five dimensions, *Bull. Amer. Math. Soc.* **66** (1960) p. 198.

19. E C Zeeman, *Geometry and perspective*, Video and booklet, Royal Institution, London, 1987.

20. E C Zeeman, Sudden changes in perception, *Logos et Théorie des Catastrophes* (ed. J Petitot), Edition Patino, Geneva (1988) pp. 279-309.